THE VCs OF WALES AND THE WELSH REGIMENTS

The VCs of Wales and the Welsh Regiments

W. Alister Williams

BRIDGE BOOKS, WREXHAM, CLWYD.

First published in Great Britain by
Bridge Books
15 Vicarage Hill,
Wrexham,
Clywd LL13 7HW.

1984

© W. Alister Williams

ISBN 0 9508285 4 8

Typeset by Alphagraphic, London, and
printed and bound by Livesey Ltd.,
Shrewsbury, Shropshire.

To

Susan, Nicola and Mark.

'That valour lies in the eyes o' the lookers on,
And is called valour with a witness.'

BEN JOHNSON

'In valour there is hope.'

TACITUS

'No thought of flight,
None of retreat, no unbecoming deed
That argued fear; each on himself relied,
As only in his arm the moment lay
Of victory.'

JOHN MILTON

CONTENTS

INTRODUCTION

Visits to Plastirion, Caernarfonshire, as a small boy, first aroused my interest in the Victoria Cross. Before the land was purchased by my grandfather, it had been the property of General Sir Hugh Rowlands, the first Welshman to be awarded Britain's highest decoration for gallantry in the face of the enemy. A passion for history and later, an interest in research, led to my undertaking the task of producing a biography of this illustrious but now forgotten compatriot. The 'bug' had bitten me and from Sir Hugh Rowlands, I moved on to other VCs — an undertaking which eventually culminated in this volume.

This book is not a history of the Victoria Cross; that task has already been carried out by several authors more eminently suited to the task than myself. Rather, it is an attempt to produce a reference work which will answer those questions that students of the award are always asking themselves but rarely get an answer to: who was he? where did he come from? what became of him?

The men whose biographical details appear here are not all Welshmen. They are, however, all connected with the Principality either by birth, residence, death or military service. Purists would argue that those VCs awarded to the 24th Regiment of Foot before 1881 should not be included in a work of this nature as the regiment was then the 2nd Warwickshire Regiment and had no more of a territorial connection with Wales than any other regiment in the army. To exclude them would be even more confusing as the modern standard bearer of that illustrious regiment is The Royal Regiment of Wales and the regimental museum is located in Brecon, Powys. Similarly, the Queen's Dragoon Guards has, since 1959, served as the cavalry regiment for Wales.

Numerous researchers have tried to find a common link between the recipients of the coveted Cross but to no avail. Each individual is only linked to the others by the exceptionally high degree of courage which was exhibited by them all. Some writers have tried to cast doubts upon the validity of some of the awards, particularly the earlier ones. They state that those awards bear no comparison with those made in later wars. This is a futile exercise. Each award was made because the individual concerned had shown great gallantry in the eyes of his contemporaries. It is not possible to judge one act of valour against another. We will never know whether it took more or less courage to face up to a Zulu impi than it took to fight against the German SS. The only assessment which we can make today is that, in the case of all VCs, the likely outcome of the individual's action was death.

As the reader makes his way through the awards recorded in this book, it will become obvious that the citations become more detailed as the story progresses and this tends to devalue the earlier awards because of the lack of information available. This is hardly the responsibility of the man concerned and his fear, pain and courage were the same.

It might be thought by some that my attempts to locate information about all aspects of a VC's life is a case of prying into details which are of no concern to the student of military history. In defence, I would say that a man's background could have a profound effect upon his actions. The VC is not the prerogative of the young and foolhardy but has been awarded to every possible classification of society. Unfortunately, over the years, the biographical details of some VC recipients have been lost. Wherever possible, I have made use of primary sources and, as a consequence, the keen reader will discover some details which disagree with those published elsewhere. I have made every effort to ensure that the data which is reproduced here is accurate. Any errors which may have slipped through are my sole responsibility.

9

No author can claim that a book of this nature is the result of his own unaided efforts. By its very nature, it must be the compilation of knowledge from numerous individuals and organisations who have willingly given their information and time. Below, I have tried to acknowledge all those who have assisted me with my searches but I feel certain that there will be some that I have overlooked. May I express my most sincere thanks and apologies as the case may be to all who have kindly co-operated with me over the last eight years. Certain names must, however, be given prominence as their contributions have been of great general value. My gratitude must go, above all, to the eminent naval historian and novelist, John Winton, who allowed me access to the voluminous files on all recipients of the Victoria Cross prepared and researched by his late mother, Mrs. Margaret Pratt, who sadly died before being able to fulfil her ambition to write the definitive book on the subject which was to be entitled 'Aristocracy of the Brave'. Her work will not be forgotten due to the interest of others and the great generosity of her son. One of the first avenues for any VC researcher must be the files prepared during a lifetime of study by the Rev. Canon William Lummis, M.C. His kindness is well known to students of British military history and I am much in his debt for his assistance and advice. Research of this nature brings one into contact with numerous 'fellow travellers', some of whom become more than names on an envelope or voices at the end of a telephone. My searches have produced two such people – Chris Bacon and Clive Hughes. For their fellowship, advice, assistance and enthusiasm, I shall always be grateful. My sincere thanks are also extended to the following institutions, organisations and individuals: The Imperial War Museum; The National Army Museum; The National Maritime Museum; The Ministry of Defence; The Public Record Office; The British Library; The National Library of Wales; The Commonwealth War Graves Commission; The South Wales Borderers Regimental Museum; The Museum of The Welch Regiment; RHQ The Welsh Guards; RHQ The Grenadier Guards; RHQ The Coldstream Guards; The Queen's Dragoon Guards Regimental Museum; The Durham Light Infantry Museum; The Argyll and Sutherland Highlanders Regimental Museum; The Royal Green Jackets Museum; The Royal Artillery Institution; The Royal Military Academy, Sandhurst; The Royal Army Medical Corps Museum; The King's Own Yorkshire Light Infantry Museum; The Worcestershire and Sherwood Forester's Museum; The Tank Museum; The Northamptonshire Regiment Museum; RHQ The Black Watch; The Duke of Cornwall's Light Infantry Museum; The Dorset Military Museum; The Powysland Museum; Wrexham Area Library; Llanelli Public Library; The University College of North Wales Library; Edinburgh University Library; Dorset County Library; Mid-Glamorgan County Library; West Glamorgan County Library; South Glamorgan County Library; Dyfed Library Service; Somerset County Library; Merthyr Tydfil Library; Gwent County Library; Wiltshire County Library; Edinburgh City Archives; Gwent County Archivist; Carmarthen Record Office; Gwynedd Archives Service; Hereford and Worcestershire Record Office; Tyne and Wear Archivist's Department; Hampshire Record Office; Staffordshire County Museum; Borough of Blaenau Gwent; Torbay Borough Council; City of Philadelphia Department of Records; Edinburgh Academy; Holyhead County Secondary School; Eastbourne School; Sherbourne College; Marlborough College; Rugby School; Eton College; Harrow School; Magdalen College; Shrewsbury School; St. Bees School; Royal Agricultural College; Brecon Cathedral; Lt. Bryn Owen, RN (Retd.); Miss Rose Coombes, MBE; Mr. Robert Mansell; Mr. Philip Warburton-Lee; Lady Dorothy Edwards; Mr. Meirig Edwards; Mr. C. L. V. P. Evans; Miss Mary Greer;

10

Mrs. Isabel Findlay; Viscount Furness; Mr. J. L. Williams; Mr. Kenneth Williams; Mr. Gethin Davies; Mr. Edward Chapman, VC, BEM; Mrs. Mary Sullivan; Mrs. Sara Jones; Mr. A. J. D. Morgan; Mr. Edward Lewis; Lady Bettina Thomson; Mrs. Frances Douglas; Mr. Derek Weale; Mrs. Susie Weale; Mr. Charles Fox Russell; Mr. Terence Collins; Mr. O'Brian; Mrs. Freda Orr; Mr. Gus Jones; Mr. Wilfred Leonard; Major David Liddell; Mrs. Phillipa Beattie; Mr. Michael Beattie; Mr. Edward Lloyd; Mrs. Joyce Hill-Ervey; Mrs. Victoria Howard; Mr. Robert Howard; Miss Meriona Jenkins Rees; Mr. W. J. Davies; Mrs. M. Booth; Major Herbert Lloyd-Johnes, OBE, TD; Mr. Walter Ireland; Rt. Hon. Lord Justice Tasker Watkins, VC, DL; Mr. H. Bunting; Mr. Bernard Baldwin, MBE; Lt. Colonel P. J. D. Johnson, OBE; Mr. William Dodd; Mrs. Dodd; Mrs. E. Whitmill; Lt. Colonel G. C. S. Coode, MBE; Major C. J. Wilson; Mr. Stephen Morris; Mrs. Wanda Pugh; Mrs. J. Ridley; Mr. G. E. Moody; Mr. Mogg Williams; The Earl of Harewood; Mrs. S. Toogood; Mr. J. Wishart; Miss W. Hempenstall; Mr. A. J. Hallowes; Mr. Chaz Bowyer; Mr. Douglas Glover; Mr. Edward Lewis; Major B. H. Jones; Miss H. M. Birks; Mrs. V. Partridge; Mrs. G. E. Moody; Mr. Albert Finn; Miss J. Lewis; Mr. David Christie-Murray; Mr. Gordon Everson; Miss Diane Meredith; Wing Commander Frederick Carrol; Mr. Vivian Smith; Mrs. Monica Carroll; Mr. F. Birks; Mr. M. Pryce May.

W. Alister Williams, 1984.

AUTHOR'S NOTE

1. Wherever possible, citations have been included for decorations other than the Victoria Cross. Unfortunately, not all awards carried a published citation in the London Gazette and therefore a great many such details are not available.

2. In some of the early VC citations very little detail was given about the circumstances of the action for which the award was made. To help clarify the award in these cases, details have been included, after the actual citation, which provide fuller information.

3. Some of the entries lack certain background details. In most cases this is as a result of the total absence of any such data in the official military or civil records. In very few cases data has been withheld at the request of the individual concerned or his family.

4. Each entry in this book carries the sub-heading 'Location of VC'. Where the VC is held by an organisation which has display facilities, e.g. regimental museums, the entry will indicate whether the VC is held by that organisation. This does not mean that the actual VC is on public display. When a VC is held by the family, or is in a private collection, the location is not given as a matter of policy.

ABBREVIATIONS

L.G.   London Gazette.

OC   Officer Commanding.

GOC   General Officer Commanding.

RMA   Royal Military Academy, Sandhurst.

M. in D. Mention in Despatches.

ADC   Aide de Camp.

K. in A. Killed in Action.

HISTORICAL BACKGROUND

THE VICTORIA CROSS

The Victoria Cross was instituted by Royal Warrant on 29th January, 1856, as a reward for acts of valour carried out by British servicemen (or foreign nationals in the service of the British Crown) in the face of the enemy. This Warrant states that the award was to be granted "with a view to place all persons on a perfectly equal footing in relation to eligibility for the order it is hereby declared that neither rank, nor long service, nor wounds, nor any circumstances or conditions whatsoever save the merit of conspicuous bravery shall be held as sufficient qualificatin for the order." Consideration that such an award should be established stemmed from questions being asked in the House of Commons by Captain Scobell, MP, on 19th December, 1854. The idea was taken up by Prince Albert and, through him, by Queen Victoria herself.

Since the original warrant was issued there have been several amendments made. The most notable of these being: the award of VCs to members of the Honourable East India Company's forces (1857); the award of VCs to Non-Military Persons bearing arms as Volunteers (1858); the award of VCs to Local Forces in New Zealand and the Colonies and their Dependencies (1867); the award of Posthumous VCs (1902); the award of VCs to members of the Royal Air Force (1919).

Throughout the period when the Victoria Cross has existed, only 1,351 men have received the award (including one to the American Unknown Warrior of the Great War). In addition, three men have received a Bar to the award.

1st KING'S DRAGOON GUARDS

Raised in 1685 during the rebellion of the Duke of Monmouth and known as the 2nd, or Queen's, Regiment of Horse, it first saw action at the Battle of the Boyne in 1690. In 1714, the regiment became known as the King's Own Regiment of Horse and in 1746, the 1st King's Dragoon Guards. During the 18th century, it saw service throughout Europe and in 1815 was present at Waterloo. It served in the closing stages of the Crimean War and in the China, Zulu, First Boer and Second Boer Wars. During the Great War it saw action on the Western Front and was mechanised in 1937. For most of the Second World War it served in the Mediterranean area. On 1st January, 1959, the 1st King's Dragoon Guards amalgamated with the 2nd Dragoon Guards (Queen's Bays) to become the 1st Queen's Dragoon Guards. The regiment's RHQ is at Maindy Barracks, Cardiff and the museum is at Clive House, Shrewsbury.

2nd DRAGOON GUARDS (QUEEN'S BAYS)

Raised in 1685 during the rebellion of the Duke of Monmouth, and known as the 3rd Regiment of Horse, it first saw action at the Battle of the Boyne in 1690. In 1746, it became known as the 2nd, or Queen's, Regiment of Dragoon Guards (later, due to the fact that its mounts were Bay horses it became known as The Queen's Bays). During the 18th century it saw active service throughout Europe. In 1857, the regiment was sent to India where it served with distinction during the Indian Mutiny. Its next major involvement was in South Africa during the Second Boer War. It served throughout the Great War on the Western Front and began to be converted to a mechanised regiment during the mid-1930s. For most of the Second World War it served in the Mediterranean area. On 1st January, 1959, the 2nd Dragoon Guards amalgamated with the 1st King's Dragoon Guards to become the 1st Queen's Dragoon Guards. The regiment's RHQ is at Maindy Barracks, Cardiff and the museum is at Clive House, Shrewsbury.

13

THE WELSH GUARDS

The Welsh Guards are the youngest of the five regiments of Foot Guards having only been formed in 1915. During its short period of service the regiment has already earned the respect of the other regiments and has won considerable glory in both World Wars and on active service throughout the world. The RHQ is at Wellington Barracks, London.

THE ROYAL WELCH FUSILIERS

Raised in 1689, as the 23rd Regiment of Foot, it was to recruit in Wales and the border country and have its HQ at Ludlow in Shropshire. The regiment first saw action at the Battle of the Boyne in 1690. Since that time, it has served in almost every major campaign in which the British Army has been involved. Its record of service is unbroken and it has never been amalgamated with any other regiment. The RHQ is at Hightown Barracks, Wrexham and the museum is at Caernarfon Castle.

THE SOUTH WALES BORDERERS

Raised in 1689, as the 24th Regiment of Foot, it first saw active service in Ireland. It served throughout the Duke of Marlborough's campaigns against the French and later in North America and the Peninsula. At Chilianwala, India, in 1849, the 24th Foot (by this time also known as the 2nd Warwickshire Regiment), lost nearly half its strength in action against the Sikhs. Thirty years later history repeated itself at Isandlwana, Zululand where the 1st Battalion lost 423 officers and men and the 2nd Battalion a further 132 officers and men. In 1881 the regiment's territorial title was changed to The South Wales Borderers. It served with distinction throughout the two World Wars. In 1969, the regiment amalgamated with The Welch Regiment to become The Royal Regiment of Wales. The RHQ is at Maindy Barracks, Cardiff and the museum (SWB) is at Brecon Barracks, Brecon.

THE WELCH REGIMENT

Raised in 1719 as a regiment of infantry it was recruited from Out-Pensioners at the Royal Hospital, Chelsea and known as The Invalids. Its duties were to garrison Britain's coastal defences and guard prisoners of war in order that the regular line regiments could be released for foreign service. In 1751 the regiment was designated the 41st Regiment of Foot and in 1787 dropped the title Invalids when it became a regular regiment of the line. In 1756, the 24th Regiment of Foot (see South Wales Borderers above) raised a second battalion in Lincolnshire which, shortly afterwards served as marines (its title being changed to the 69th Regiment of Foot in 1758). These two regiments, 41st and 69th, served with distinction throughout the world during the 19th century and, in 1881, amalgamated to become the 1st and 2nd Battalions, The Welch Regiment. The regiment served in the Boer War and throughout the two World Wars. In 1969, the Welch Regiment amalgamated with the South Wales Borderers to become The Royal Regiment of Wales. The RHQ is at Maindy Barracks, Cardiff and the museum (Welch Regiment) is in Cardiff Castle.

SERGEANT LUKE O'CONNOR
23rd Regiment of Foot

Full Name: Luke O'Connor.

Place of Birth: Elphine, County Roscommon, Ireland.

Date of Birth: 20th February, 1831.

Father: —

Mother: —

Father's Occupation: —

Education: —

Pre-Service Employment: —

Service Record: Enlisted as a Private, 23rd Regiment of Foot, 21st July, 1849; Corporal, 15th May, 1850; Sergeant, 18th May, 1851; Colour Sergeant, 22nd September, 1854; served Crimean Campaign, 1854-56 (present at the Alma and during the Siege of Sebastopol), severely wounded 20th September, 1854; dangerously wounded 8th September, 1855; commissioned as an Ensign, 76th Regiment of Foot, 19th October, 1854 (without purchase as a reward for his gallant conduct at the Battle of the Alma); exchanged to 23rd Regiment of Foot, 5th November, 1854; Lieutenant, 9th February, 1855 (without purchase); served Indian Mutiny 1857-8 (present at the relief and capture of Lucknow); Captain, 24th August, 1858 (without purchase); served Gibraltar, 1863-66; served Canada, 1866-67; Brevet-Major, 5th July, 1872; served Ashanti War, 1873-74; served Gibraltar, 1874-80; Major, 19th August, 1874; Brevet Lieutenant Colonel, 1st April, 1874; Lieutenant Colonel, 21st June, 1880; Colonel, 17th August, 1879; half-pay, 1886; retired 2nd March, 1887; Hon. Major General, 9th March, 1887; Colonel Royal Welch Fusiliers, 3rd June, 1914.

Rewards, Decorations and Medals: Victoria Cross (for action at the Battle of the Alma, 20th September, 1854 and before Sebastopol, 8th September, 1855); CB (L.G. 29th June, 1906); KCB (L.G. 3rd June, 1913); Crimea Medal (clasps for Alma and Sebastopol); Indian Mutiny Medal (clasps for Relief of Lucknow and Lucknow); Ashanti War Medal, 1873-74 (no clasps); Turkish Order of the Medjidie, 5th Class (1856); Turkish Crimea Medal; Sardinian Crimea Medal; received the thanks of Sir George Brown and Sir William Codrington on the field of the Alma (1854); Reward for Distinguished Service; received one year's pay as Lieutenant and a temporary pension as Brevet Lieutenant Colonel for his services during the Ashanti Campaign of 1873-74.

Post-Service Employment: Retired General Officer. Hon. Colonel Royal Welch Fusiliers.

Married: Not married.

Children: None.

Died: Clarges Street, London, 1st February, 1915.

Buried: Plot 1100, St. Mary's R.C. Cemetery, Kensal Rise, London, 4th February, 1915.

Memorials: St. Mary's R.C. Cemetery, Kensal Rise, London. Portrait R.W.F. Museum, Caernarfon.

Location of VC: R.W.F. Museum, Caernarfon Castle.

Citation for VC: L.G. 24th February, 1857.

"Was one of the centre Sergeants at the Battle of the Alma and advanced between the Officers carrying the colours. When near the Redoubt, Lieutenant Anstruther, who was carrying a Colour, was mortally wounded and he was shot in the breast at the same time and fell, but recovering himself, snatched up the Colour from the ground, and continued to carry it till the end of the action although urged by Captain Granville to relinquish it and go to the rear on account of his wound; was recommended for and received his commission for his services at the Alma (September 20th, 1854). Also behaved with great gallantry at the assault on the Redan 8th September, 1855, where he was shot through both thighs."

He was decorated with the VC by H.M. Queen Victoria at the first VC Investiture held in Hyde Park, London, 26th June, 1857.

N.B. Luke O'Connor's action was the first for which the VC was awarded to a member of the British Army although, because of the reference to the award being made for two events, twelve months apart, this honour has been claimed by others.

CAPTAIN EDWARD BELL
23rd Regiment of Foot

Full Name: Edward William Derrington Bell.

Place of Birth: Landguard Fort, Essex. The family home was The Lodge, Kempsey, Worcestershire.

Date of Birth: Not known. He was baptised on 19th January, 1824.

Father: Lieutenant General Edward Wells Bell (late Royal Fusiliers).

Mother: Marianne Bell.

Father's Occupation: General Officer.

Education: Sandhurst School; RMA Sandhurst.

Service Record: Commissioned as an Ensign, 23rd Regiment of Foot, 15th April, 1842; Lieutenant, 17th November, 1843; Captain, 18th December, 1848; served Crimean Campaign, 1854-56 (present at the Alma, Inkerman and Sebastopol); Brevet Major, 12th December, 1854; Major, 23rd March, 1855; Brevet Lieutenant Colonel, 26th December, 1856; served Indian Mutiny (present at the capture of Lucknow) 1857-58; Lieutenant Colonel, 30th March, 1858; Colonel, 10th August, 1862; Major General, 6th March, 1868; GOC Belfast District, 28th February, 1875.

Rewards, Decorations and Medals: Victoria Cross (for action at the Battle of the Alma, 20th September, 1854); CB; Crimean Medal (clasps for Alma, Inkerman and Sebastopol); Indian Mutiny Medal (clasp for Lucknow); Turkish Crimea Medal; Turkish Order of the Medjidie, 5th Class (1856); Legion of Honour, 5th Class (1856); MinD (Crimea and Indian Mutiny); Reward for Distinguished Service.

Married: Charlotte Wadsworth Davies (widow of Surgeon Davies) nee Bartell, at St. Mary's Church, Cheltenham, 3rd August, 1869. She was the daughter of Robert Wadsworth Bartell, Esq. At the time of his marriage, Bell resided at 33, The Promenade, Cheltenham.

Children: One son and three daughters.

Died: Lisbreen House, Fort William Park, Belfast, Ireland, 10th November, 1879.

Buried: Kempsey Churchyard, Kempsey, Worcestershire.

Location of VC: Believed to be held by the family.

Citation for VC: L.G. 24th February, 1857.

"Recommended for his gallantry, more particularly at the Battle of the Alma, where he was the first to seize upon and capture one of the enemy's guns which was limbered up and being carried off. He moreover, succeeded to the command of that gallant regiment which he brought out of action; all his senior officers having been killed or wounded."

He was decorated with the VC by H.M. Queen Victoria on Southsea Common, Hampshire, 2nd August, 1858.

SERGEANT AMBROSE MADDEN
41st Regiment of Foot

Full Name: Ambrose Madden.

Place of Birth: Cork, Ireland.

Date of Birth: Circa 1820.

Father: —

Mother: —

Father's Occupation: —

Education: —

Pre-Service Employment: Labourer.

Service Record: Enlisted 2nd Dragoon Guards at Cahir, 24th May, 1838 (Service No. 550); transferred to 41st Regiment of Foot at Dublin, 31st October, 1845 (Service No. 2195); Corporal, 16th June, 1848; Sergeant, 7th September, 1849; Colour Sergeant, 1st May, 1853; served Crimean Campaign, 1854-56 (present at Alma, Little Inkerman, Inkerman and Sebastopol); Acting Sergeant Major, 7th August, 1855; Sergeant Major, 2nd October, 1856; resigned and reverted to Colour Sergeant, 12th October, 1858; voluntary transfer to 2nd West India Regiment, 31st October, 1858; Company Sergeant Major, 1st November, 1858; Commissioned Ensign, 2nd West India Regiment, 13th December, 1858; served in Baddiboo War, West Africa, 1861 (present at the bombardment of Sowarracunda Creek, 16th February, 1861, the storming and capture of Carawan, Kinty Cunda and Saba) where he suffered a severe attack of fever but continued to carry out his duties; Lieutenant, 20th August, 1861; transferred to 3rd West India Regiment, April, 1861, as Garrison Adjutant at Gambia, West Africa; transferred to 4th West India Regiment, 7th April, 1862.

Rewards, Decoration and Medals: Victoria Cross (for action at Little Inkerman, 26th October, 1854); Crimean Medal (clasps for Alma, Inkerman and Sebastopol); French Medaille Militaire; Turkish Crimea Medal.

Married: Bridget Furlong at Tuam, Galway, Ireland, 10th September, 1847.

Children: Two daughters.

Died: Jamaica, 1st January, 1863, of fever.

Buried: Location of grave not known.

Memorials: None recorded.

Location of VC: Welch Regiment Museum, Cardiff Castle.

Citation for VC: L.G. 24th February, 1857.

"For having headed a party of men of the 41st Regiment and having cut off and taken prisoner one Russian officer and fourteen privates, three of

17

whom he personally and alone captured."

He was decorated with the VC by Major General E. W. Bell, Lieutenant Governor and GOC Jamaica, 7th August, 1857.

CAPTAIN HUGH ROWLANDS
41st Regiment of Foot

Full Name: Hugh Rowlands.

Place of Birth: Plastirion, Llanrug, nr. Caernarfon, Caernarfonshire.

Date of Birth: 6th May, 1828.

Father: John Rowlands.

Mother: Elizabeth Anne Rowlands (nee Hastwell).

Father's Occupation: Gentleman landowner. Deputy Lieutenant of Caernarfonshire, Justice of the Peace, officer in the Caernarfonshire Militia.

Education: Beaumaris Grammar School, Anglesey, 1837-1842; Mr. John Taylor's Cramming Academy, Woolwich, July-August, 1849.

Service Record: Commissioned Ensign in the 41st Regiment of Foot, 25th September, 1849 (by purchase); Lieutenant, 21st April, 1851; Captain, Grenadier Company, 24th August, 1854 (by purchase); served Crimean Campaign (present at the Alma, Little Inkerman, Inkerman and throughout the siege of Sebastopol); wounded severely in the arm at Inkerman and slightly during the second assault on the Redan, September, 1855; Brevet Major, 2nd November, 1855; Town Major of Sebastopol, September, 1855; Brigade Major, 2nd Brigade, 2nd Division, Sebastopol, 1st October, 1855; Major, 13th December, 1857; half pay, 6th November, 1857; Staff Major at Aldershot, July, 1858; Major 3/7th Regiment at Chatham, August, 1858; half-pay, 26th August, 1859; Major, 100th Regiment, December, 1860; Major, 41st Regiment, 5th February, 1861; Brevet Lieutenant Colonel, May, 1865; Lieutenant Colonel, 41st Regiment, 23rd March, 1866; Colonel, 23rd March, 1871; O.C. 1st Border Regiment, 12th May, 1875; Special Service Officer, Cape Colony, March, 1878; Inspector of Colonial Forces, Transvaal, May, 1878; Commandant of the Transvaal, 13th August, 1878; O.C. campaign against the Bapedi in Eastern Transvaal, 1878; O.C. No. 5 Column, Transvaal, January, 1879; O.C. defences of Pretoria from threat of Boer attack, March, 1879; Brigadier (temporary rank), 21st May, 1879; GOC, Brigade Lower Tugela River, Natal, June, 1879; half-pay, August, 1879; A.A.Q.M.G., North British District, 1st July, 1880; Brigadier General, Peshawar Brigade, Bengal, January, 1881; Major General, 1st July, 1881; GOC, 3rd Infantry Brigade, Aldershot, 19th August, 1882; GOC, Bangalore Division, Madras, 21st April, 1884; GOC (temporary), Madras Army, August, 1885-March, 1886 and October, 1886-December, 1886; unattached officer, April, 1889; Lieutenant General, 1st January, 1890; Lieutenant of the Tower of London, 21st June, 1893; GOC, Scottish District, 5th January, 1894; General, 16th October, 1894; Retired, 6th May, 1896; Colonel, Duke of Wellington's (West Riding) Regiment, 8th October, 1897.

Rewards, Decorations and Medals: Victoria Cross (for action at Inkerman, 5th November, 1854); KCB (L.G. 24th May, 1898), CB (L.G. 29th May, 1875, for services in the Crimean War); Reward for Distinguished Service (31st January, 1880, for services in South Africa, 1878-79); Crimean Medal (with clasps for Alma, Inkerman and Sebastopol); South Africa Medal

18

(with clasp for 1878-9); M. in D. (Crimea and South Africa); Legion of Honour (21st June, 1856); Order of the Medjidie (1856); Turkish Crimea Medal; Deputy Lieutenant of Caernarfonshire; Justice of the Peace (Caernarfon and the Transvaal).

Post-Service Employment: Retired General Officer, landowner, Justice of the Peace.

Married: Isabella Jane Barrow (daughter of Thomas James Raikes Barrow, RN, of Randwick, Stroud, Gloucester) at Serampore, India, 2nd November, 1867.

Children: One daughter and one son (son later died of wounds received whilst serving as a Major in the King's African Rifles, in Somaliland in 1903).

Died: 1st August, 1909, at his home, Plastirion, Llanrug, Caernarfonshire.

Buried: St. Michael's Churchyard, Llanrug, Caernarfonshire.

Memorials: St. Michael's Churchyard, Llanrug, Caernarfonshire.

Location of VC: Museum of the Welch Regiment, Cardiff Castle.

Citation for VC: L.G. 24th February, 1857.
"For having rescued Colonel Haly, of the 47th Regiment, from Russian soldiers, Colonel Haly having been wounded and surrounded by them, and for gallant exertions in holding the ground occupied by his advanced picquet against the enemy, at the commencement of the Battle of Inkerman."
He was decorated with the VC by Major General Sir A. Josias Cloete, at Barbados, 5th August, 1857.

N.B. Of interest with this award is the fact that Rowlands was nominated for a second VC for his action during the abortive assault on the Redan on 18th June, 1855.

PRIVATE JOHN BYRNE
1/68th Light Infantry

Full Name: John Byrne.

Place of Birth: Castlecomber, Kilkenny, Ireland.

Date of Birth: Circa September, 1832.

Father: —

Mother: —

Father's Occupation: —

Education: No education certificate. His signature was very clumsy which would seem to indicate that he was probably illiterate.

Pre-Service Employment: —

Service Record: Enlisted 68th Light Infantry at Coventry, 27th July, 1850 (Service No. 2832); served Crimean Campaign, 1854-56 (present at Alma, Inkerman, Balaclava and Sebastopol), slightly wounded in the foot 13th January, 1855; Corporal, 21st January, 1861; Sergeant, 7th March, 1866; served East Indies and in New Zealand during the Maori War, 1860-66; discharged at Cork, 14th May, 1869; served as Sergeant, Queen's County Militia, May-October, 1869; re-enlisted 68th Light Infantry, October, 1869 as a Sergeant; discharged, 14th May, 1872; served as Colour Sergeant, North Durham Militia, 1872, believed to have been discharged in the same year " . . . for insubordination and highly improper conduct."

Rewards, Decorations and Medals: Victoria Cross (for action at Inkerman, 5th

19

November, 1854, and in the trenches before Sebastopol, 11th May, 1855); Distinguished Conduct Medal (for action at Tauranga, New Zealand, 27th June, 1864); Crimea Medal (clasps for Alma, Balaclava, Inkerman and Sebastopol); New Zealand Medal, 1861-66; Turkish Crimea Medal; 3 Good Conduct Badges (he would have received four had he not been promoted and five had he served a further five days and not been promoted).

Post-Service Employment: Little information is available on this period of his life. When he left the army his intended place of residence was given as Durham. In 1878 he obtained employment in Bristol as a labourer with the Ordnance Survey.

Married: No record of marriage.

Children: None.

Died: On 10th July, 1879, whilst working for the Ordnance Survey at Caerleon, Monmouthshire, Byrne entered into an argument with a man named John Watts with whom he worked. It was reported that Watts had insulted the Victoria Cross. Byrne pulled out a revolver and fired at Watts but missed. Later the same day, a police officer called at 7 Crown Street, Maindee (where Byrne was lodging) to question him about the incident. Byrne again drew out the pistol, placed the barrel in his mouth and fired. He died instantly. The inquest held two days later recorded a verdict of suicide whilst of unsound mind.

Buried: Grave R.C. E15, Block 14, St. Woolo's Cemetery, Newport, 12th July, 1879. This is part of the lawn cemetery and is unmarked.

Memorials: None recorded.

Location of VC: Not known. His New Zealand Medal is held by the Durham Light Infantry Museum.

Citation for VC: L.G. 24th February, 1857.
"At the Battle of Inkerman, when the regiment was ordered to retire, Private John Byrne went back towards the enemy, and, at the risk of his own life, brought in a wounded soldier, under fire.
"On the 11th May, 1855, he bravely engaged in a hand to hand contest with one of the enemy on the parapet of the work he was defending, prevented the entrance of the enemy, killed his antagonist, and captured his arms."

He was decorated with the VC by Major General Sir George Buller, GOC Ionian Islands, at Corfu, 22nd July, 1857.

Citation for DCM: L.G. 16th September, 1864.
There is no actual citation for this award but the despatch from which it originates was published in the London Gazette on the above date:
"Corporal J. Byrne, VC (68th) who, when the order to charge was given, was the first man of his company into the rifle pits. A maori whom he transfixed with his bayonet seized his rifle with one hand and holding it firm with the bayonet through him, this time endeavoured to cut him down with his tomahawk and his life was saved by Sergeant Murray."

N.B. The Sergeant Murray who saved Byrne's life was decorated with the VC for his gallantry. It was believed that John Byrne had died on 6th December, 1872, until the discovery of the events in South Wales.

COMMANDER HENRY RABY, R.N.
Naval Brigade, Crimea

Full Name: Henry James Raby.

Place of Birth: Boulogne, France, 26th September, 1827. The Raby family had no permanent address at this time and were travelling to Germany. Previously, they had lived at Brynmor, Llanelli, Carmarthenshire, where Henry's father and grandfather had various industrial interests.

Father: Arthur Tournour Raby.

Mother: —

Father's Occupation: Industrialist (metal and coal industries), Llanelli, Carmarthenshire.

Education: Sherborne School, 1840-41.

Service Record: Entered Royal Navy as a 1st Class Volunteer, HMS Monarch, 8th March, 1842; paid off 28th October, 1843; Midshipman, HMS Rodney, 7th March, 1848; Sub-Lieutenant, HMS Ocean, 30th March, 1849; Sub-Lieutenant, HMS Terrible, 23rd November, 1849; Lieutenant, 15th January, 1850; discharged to half-pay (shore), 13th January, 1850; Lieutenant, HMS Wasp, West Africa Station, 2nd October, 1850; Lieutenant, HMS Wasp, Circassia, in support of Turkish Army, January, 1854; Lieutenant, HMS Diamond, 24th October, 1854; landed with the Naval Brigade in the Crimea, October, 1854, present at Inkerman, 5th November, 1854; served in the trenches before Sebastopol, 1854-55; second-in-command of ladder party during assault on the Redan, 18th June, 1855; Commander, 29th September, 1855 (for services rendered during the siege of Sebastopol); OC, HMS Medusa, West Africa Station on anti-slavery operations, 1857; OC, HMS Alecto, West Africa Station, anti-slavery operation, 1859-62; took command of the squadron's boats at the capture of Porto Novo, April, 1861 (wounded); promoted Captain, 24th November, 1862 (for services rendered in West Africa); OC, HMS Adventurer, China Station, 1868-71; retired from the Service, 27th September, 1877; Rear-Admiral (Retired List), 21st March, 1878.

Rewards, Decorations and Medals: Victoria Cross (for action during the assault on the Redan at Sebastopol, 18th June, 1855); CB (1875); Crimean Medal (with clasps for Inkerman and Sebastopol); Legion of Honour, 3rd Class (1856); Order of the Medjidie, 4th Class (1856); Turkish Crimea Medal; Sardinian Crimea Medal; M. in D. (Crimea and West Africa); Reward for Distinguished Service.

Post-Service Employment: Retired Rear-Admiral. Committee member for the Royal Sailors' Home, Portsmouth, and South Hampshire School and Home for the Blind.

Married: Judith, daughter of Thomas Watkin Foster of Holt Manor, Trowbridge, Wiltshire, 31st December, 1863.

Children: Three sons.

Died: 13th February, 1907, at his home, 8 Clarence Parade, Southsea, Hampshire.

Buried: Highland Road Cemetery, Portsmouth.

Memorials: Highland Road Cemetery, Portsmouth; a road in Llanelli, Carmarthenshire is named after his family which was instrumental in bringing industrialisation to the town.

Location of VC: Royal Naval Museum, Portsmouth.

Citation for VC: L.G. 24th February, 1857.

"On the 18th June, 1855, immediately after the assault on Sebastopol, a soldier of the 57th Regiment, who had been shot through both legs, was observed sitting up and calling for assistance. Climbing over the breastwork of the advanced sap, Commander Raby and two seamen (John Taylor and Henry Curtis) proceeded upwards of 70 yards across open space towards the salient angle of the Redan, and in spite of the heavy fire which was still continuing, succeeded in carrying the wounded soldier to a place of safety, at imminent risk of their own lives."

He was decorated with the VC by H.M. Queen Victoria at the first VC investiture held in Hyde Park, London, 26th June, 1857. As the most senior officer of the senior service to receive the Cross he became the first man ever to wear the VC.

N.B. The two men who were involved in the rescue with Raby, John Taylor and Henry Curtis, were both awarded the VC for the same action. Sadly, Taylor died on 24th February, 1857, the very day that the citation appeared in the London Gazette.

CAPTAIN CHARLES LUMLEY
97th (Earl of Ulster's) Regiment

Full Name: Charles Henry Lumley.

Place of Birth: Forres House, Forres, Morayshire. He also resided at Shooter's Hill, London.

Date of Birth: Circa 1824.

Father: —

Mother: —

Father's Occupation: —

Education: —

Service Record: Commissioned Ensign, 97th Regiment of Foot, 30th August, 1844; promoted Lieutenant, 18th February, 1848; promoted Captain, 29th December, 1854; served Crimean Campaign 1855-56 (siege of Sebastopol, second assault of the Redan, 8th September, 1855, severely wounded in the head); Brevet Major, 2nd November, 1855; half-pay, 4th September, 1857; Major, 4th December, 1857; unattached Major, 1857-8; transferred to 2/23rd Regiment of Foot, 1858; OC, 2/23rd Regiment detachment at Brecon, 20th July, 1858.

Rewards, Decorations and Medals: Victoria Cross (for action during the assault on the Redan, Sebastopol, 8th September, 1855); Crimean Medal (clasp for Sebastopol); Turkish Crimea Medal; Legion of Honour.

Married: No record of any marriage.

Children: None recorded.

Died: Shot himself in the head at Brecon, 17th October, 1858, and died a few hours later. An inquest which met eight days later gave a verdict of suicide due to temporary insanity.

Buried: Brecon Cathedral, Brecon (N.E. corner of the churchyard).

Memorials: Brecon Cathedral Churchyard, Brecon.

Location of VC: In a private collection. Lumley's other medals are in the Museum of the Queen's Own Loyal West Kents at Maidstone in Kent.

Citation for VC: L.G. 24th February, 1857.

"For having distinguished himself highly by his bravery at the assault on the Redan, 8th September, 1855, being among the first inside the work, where he was immediately engaged with three Russian gunners reloading a field piece, who attacked him; he shot two of them with his revolver, when he was knocked down by a stone, which stunned him for a moment, but, on recovery, he drew his sword, and was in the act of cheering the men on, when he received a ball in the mouth, which wounded him most severely."

He was decorated with the VC by H.M. Queen Victoria at the first VC investiture held in Hyde Park, London, 26th June, 1857.

ASSISTANT SURGEON WILLIAM SYLVESTER
23rd Regiment of Foot

Full Name: William Henry Thomas Sylvester.

Place of Birth: Long Street, Devizes, Wiltshire.

Date of Birth: 19th April, 1831.

Father: Charles Sylvester.

Mother: Elizabeth Sylvester.

Father's Occupation: Surgeon.

Education: Marischal University, Aberdeen (MB, 1853, and MD, 1855), Edinburgh University (LRCS, 1853, and LSA, 1869).

Service Record: Appointed Assistant Surgeon (Staff), 3rd March, 1854; Assistant Surgeon, 23rd Regiment of Foot, Royal Welch Fusiliers, 22nd September, 1854; served Crimean Campaign (siege of Sebastopol); served Indian Mutiny 1857-8 (Relief of Lucknow); Surgeon (Staff), 10th July, 1860; retired from the army, 15th November, 1861 (due to a spinal disease which he had contracted whilst in India. This resulted in a stooped back for the remainder of his life).

Rewards, Decorations and Medals: Victoria Cross (for action at the Redan, Sebastopol, 8th September, 1855); Crimea Medal (clasp for Sebastopol); Indian Mutiny Medal (clasps for Relief of Lucknow and Lucknow); M. in D. (Crimea); Turkish Crimea Medal; Legion of Honour (5th Class).

Post-Service Employment: After leaving the army, Dr. Sylvester was appointed House Surgeon at Swansea Hospital, Glamorgan. He later served as Chief Medical Officer to Millbank Prison in London and had a private practice in Westminster at 7, Bessborough Gardens.

Married: Martha Elizabeth Watson, 7th May, 1874 (she had been a nurse at Swansea Hospital). At the time of his marriage he resided at 66, Bessborough Street, Westminster, London.

Children: Two daughters.

Died: 13th March, 1920, at his home 8, Beach Road, Paignton, Devon.

Buried: Paignton Cemetery, 18th March, 1920. Grave No. 2614.

Memorials: Paignton Cemetery, Devon.

Location of VC: RAMC Museum, Aldershot.

Citation for VC: L.G. 20th November, 1857.

"For going out on 8th September, 1855, under a heavy fire in front of the fifth parallel Right Attack, to a spot near the Redan, where Lieutenant and Adjutant Dyneley was lying mortally wounded and for dressing his wounds in that dangerous and exposed situation. N.B. This officer was mentioned in General Simpson's despatch of 18th September, 1855, for going to the front under heavy fire to assist the wounded."

Decorated with the VC by H.M. Queen Victoria at the first VC investiture held in Hyde Park, London, on 26th June, 1857.

N.B. Sylvester worked with Florence Nightingale at Scutari Hospital during the Crimean War. See also Corporal Robert Shields, VC.

CORPORAL ROBERT SHIELDS
23rd Regiment of Foot

Full Name: Robert Shields.

Place of Birth: Hope and Anchor Inn, 41, St. Mary's Street, Cardiff.

Date of Birth: Not known but he was baptised on 26th August, 1827.

Father: John Shields.

Mother: Anne Shields.

Father's Occupation: Mason later a publican.

Education: —

Pre-Service Employment: Moulder.

Service Record: Enlisted in the 23rd Regiment of Foot, Royal Welch Fusiliers, 9th April, 1847 (Service No. 2945); served in the Crimean Campaign 1854-56, present at the Battle of Inkerman and during the siege of Sebastopol; promoted Corporal, 9th September, 1855; bought his discharge for £15, 6th December, 1856.

Rewards, Decorations and Medals: Victoria Cross (for action during the assault on the Redan, Sebastopol, 8th September, 1855); Crimean Medal (with clasps for Inkerman and Sebastopol); Legion of Honour; Cambrian Torque of Valour (presented to him at the Llangollen National Esiteddfod, 1858); Turkish Crimean Medal.

Post-Service Employment: Park Ranger circa 1857 (possibly Regent's Park, London); he is referred to as a "Gate Keeper" in Queen Victoria's Journal for 26th June, 1857. In 1864, he emigrated to Bombay, India, where he was employed as an Overseer by the Back Bay Reclamation Company.

Married: Elizabeth Anne Crewe (schoolmistress) on 23rd April, 1857.

Children: None recorded.

Died: Bombay, India, 23rd December, 1864.

Buried: Location of grave is not known.

Memorials: None recorded.

Location of VC: Not known.

Citation for VC: L.G. 24th February, 1857.

"For volunteering, on 8th September, 1855, to go out to the front from the 5th parallel after the attack on the Redan, to bring in Lieutenant Dyneley, who was wounded and found afterwards to be mortally so."

He was decorated with the VC by H.M. Queen Victoria at the first VC investiture in Hyde Park, London, on 26th June, 1857.

N.B. See also Assistant Surgeon William Sylvester, VC.

2nd LIEUTENANT JAMES HILLS
Bengal Horse Artillery

Full Name: James Hills (he adopted the surname Hills-Johnes, by Royal Licence, after his marriage).

Place of Birth: Neechindipore, Bengal, India.

Date of Birth: 20th August, 1833.

Father: James Hills.

Mother: Charlotte Hills, daughter of Signor Angelo Savi of Moisgunge, Bengal, India.

Father's Occupation: Indigo Planter.

Education: Edinburgh Academy, 1843-47; Military College, Edinburgh; Addiscombe, 1851-53. At this time the family lived at Dean Bank House, Edinburgh.

Service Record: Commissioned 2nd Lieutenant, Bengal Artillery, 11th June, 1853; Lieutenant, 8th September, 1857; served Indian Mutiny, 1857-8 (present at the actions at Hindun River, May 1857, Budlee-ke-serai, June, 1857, occupation of Delhi Ridge, June, 1857, Nujufghur, 25th August, 1857, assault and capture of Delhi, September, 1857, severely wounded, July, 1857, Fort Rooiya, April, 1858, Bareilly, May, 1858, relief of Shahjehanpur, May, 1858, and Mohmundee); ADC to Lord Canning, Governor General and Viceroy of India, September, 1859-March, 1862; Captain, 24th November, 1860; Assistant Resident in Nepal, April, 1862-March, 1863; Brevet Major, 19th January, 1864; Brigade Major, RA Northern Division, Bengal, September, 1864-69; served Eusofzai Expedition, 1863-64; served Abyssinian Expedition, 1867-68 (present, as OC Mortars, at the capture of Magdala); Brevet Lieutenant Colonel, 15th August, 1868; OC Peshawar Mountain Battery, 1869; OC Kohat District, February, 1870-April, 1871; served Lushai Expedition, 1871-72; OC 'C' Battery, RHA, 1st August, 1872-75; Brevet Colonel, 14th February, 1876; AAG Lahore Division, July, 1876-August, 1879; AAG to General Stewart, Kandahar Field Force, 1878-80 (present at Patko Shano, defence of Kandahar, Kurram Valley, Charasiah Sherpur and occupation of Kabul); Major General, 10th July, 1879; Military Governor of Kabul, 13th October, 1879-17th January, 1880; unemployed, 18th January, 1880-15th May, 1880; GOC 3rd Division, Northern Afghanistan Field Force, 16th May, 1880-September, 1880; Lieutenant General, 31st December, 1883; retired, 1888; Hon. Colonel Carmarthenshire Artillery, 1891-1907; Hon. Colonel Pembrokeshire Volunteer Bn. and 4th Bn. The Welch Regiment, 1909.

Rewards, Decorations and Medals: Victoria Cross (for action during the siege of Delhi, 9th July, 1857); Indian Mutiny Medal (clasps for Delhi and Lucknow); Abyssinian Medal, 1867-68; Indian General Service Medal, 1852-95 (clasp for Looshai); Afghan War Medal, 1878-80 (clasps for Charasia and Kabul); M. in D. (Indian Mutiny, Lushai Campaign and Abyssinian Campaign); received the thanks of the Governor General of India for his services in Kabul (1880); received the thanks of both Houses of Parliament for his services in Kabul (1880); CB (L.G. 10th September, 1872); KCB (L.G. 22nd February, 1881); GCB (L.G. 2nd June, 1893); LL.D. (University of Wales); Freeman of the County and Borough of Carmarthen (1910); High Sheriff of Carmarthenshire (1886); Deputy Lieutenant of Carmarthenshire; Justice of the Peace.

Post-Service Employment: County Councillor for Carmarthenshire; Member of the Council of the University College of Wales, Aberystwyth; Member of the University Court, Aberystwyth; Treasurer of the University College of Wales, Aberystwyth; he accompanied Field Marshal Lord Roberts, VC, to South Africa (in a civilian capacity) during the Boer War.

Married: Elizabeth, daughter of John Johnes Esq., of Dolaucothy, Carmarthenshire at Westminster Abbey, London, 16th September, 1882.

Children: None.

Died: At his home at Dolaucothy, Carmarthenshire, 3rd January, 1919.

Buried: Caio Churchyard, Carmarthenshire.

Memorials: Caio Church, Carmarthenshire, and portrait in Edinburgh Academy, Edinburgh.

Location of VC: Held, on loan, by the Royal Artillery Institution.

Citation for VC: L.G. 27th April, 1858.

"For very gallant conduct on the part of Lieutenant Hills before Delhi, in defending the position assigned to him in case of alarm, and for noble behaviour on the part of Lieutenant Colonel Tombs in twice coming to his subaltern's rescue, and on each time killing his man."

He was decorated with the VC by Sir Colin Campbell, C. in C. India, 1858.

N.B. The full background to this VC award can be seen in Lt. Colonel Mackenzie's despatch of 10th July, 1857: " . . . Second-Lieut. J. Hills was on picket-duty, with two guns, at the mound to the right of the camp. About eleven o'clock a.m. there was a rumour that the enemy's cavalry were coming down on this post. Lieut. Hills proceeded to take up the position assigned in case of alarm, but before he reached the spot he saw the enemy close upon his guns, before he had time to form up. To enable him to do this, Lieut. Hills boldly charged, single-handed, the head of the enemy's column, cut down the first man, struck the second and was then ridden down, horse and all. On getting up and searching for his sword, three more men came at him (two mounted). The first man he wounded with his pistol, he caught the lance of the second with his left hand, and wounded him with his sword. The first man then came on again and was cut down; the third man (on foot) then came up and wrenched the sword from the hand of Lieut. Hills (who fell in the struggle), and the enemy was about to cut him down when Major Tombs . . . saw what was going on, rushed in and shot the man and saved Lieut. Hills. By this time the enemy's cavalry had passed by . . . Lieut. Hills observed one of the enemy passing with his (Lieut. Hills') pistol. They walked towards him. The man began flourishing his sword and dancing about. He first cut at Lieut. Hills, who parried the blow, and then he turned on Major Tombs, who received the blow in the same manner. His second attack on Lieut. Hills was, I regret to say, more successful, as he was cut down with a bad sword cut on the head, and would no doubt have been killed had not Major Tombs rushed in and put his sword through the man."

N.B. Major Henry Tombs was also awarded the VC for his gallantry in saving the life of Hills.

BOMBADIER JACOB THOMAS
Bengal Artillery, Indian Army

Full Name: Jacob Thomas.

Place of Birth: Coed-Y-Bwddy Farm, Llanwinio, Carmarthenshire.

Date of Birth: Circa February, 1833.

Father: Jacob Thomas.

Mother: —

Father's Occupation: Farmer and carpenter.

Education: —

Pre-Service Employment: Fitter-up.

Service Record: Enlisted in the Artillery at Cardiff for 12 years' service, 6th July, 1853; sailed for Bengal for service with the East India Company Artillery, 1853; Bombadier, 1st August, 1857; served Indian Mutiny 1857-8 (present at the defence of Lucknow); Corporal, 6th August, 1858; Sergeant, 29th March, 1859; transferred to the Royal Artillery, 12th June, 1861, served with the 16th Brigade RA in India; Hospital Sergeant, 1st February, 1862; Battery Sergeant, 7th March, 1863; Quarter Master Sergeant, 23rd March, 1863-14th November, 1865; took his discharge (unfit for further service) at Darjeeling, India, 30th October, 1866; granted a pension due to injuries sustained when a horse fell on him.

Rewards, Decorations and Medals: Victoria Cross (for action at Lucknow, 27th September, 1857); Indian Mutiny Medal (clasps for Defence of Lucknow and Lucknow).

Post-Service Employment: There is some confusion regarding Thomas' life after he left the army. The records of two men, both named Jacob Thomas, seem to fit him. The first joined the local police force and rose to become a Police Inspector in Darjeeling. The second was employed as a fitter at Hooghly. The evidence would seem to indicate that Jacob Thomas, VC, was the latter (he had been a fitter before joining the army).

Married: Margaret Hamilton (widow), daughter of Alexander Taggart at St. James' Church, Delhi, 14th March, 1859.

Children: None recorded.

Died: 24th April, 1896, at Hooghly, India (if the VC was the 'fitter' referred to above), or 3rd March, 1911, at Darjeeling (if he was the Police Inspector).

Buried: 24th April, 1896, at Bandel Church, Hooghly, India (if the 'fitter' referred to above).

Memorials: —

Location of VC: 55th (The Residency) Field Battery, Royal Artillery.

Citation for VC: L.G. 24th December, 1858.

"For distinguished gallantry at Lucknow on 27th September, 1857, in having brought off his own back, under a heavy fire, under circumstances of considerable difficulty, a wounded soldier of the Madras Fusiliers, when the party to which he was attached was returning to the Residency from a sortie, whereby he saved him from falling into the hands of the enemy."

He was decorated with the VC by H.M. Queen Victoria at Windsor, 4th January, 1860.

CAPTAIN, THE HON. AUGUSTUS ANSON
2/84th Regiment

Full Name: Augustus Henry Archibald Anson.

Place of Birth: Slebech Hall, Pembrokeshire.

Date of Birth: 5th March, 1835.

Father: Thomas William Anson, 1st Earl of Lichfield, 2nd Viscount Anson, of Strugborough and Orgleave, Staffordshire.

Mother: Louisa Catherine Anson (nee Philips of Slebech Hall, Pembrokeshire).

Father's Occupation: Peer of the Realm, Landowner.

Education: —

Service Record: Commissioned as an Ensign, Rifle Brigade, 27th May, 1853; Lieutenant, 8th December, 1854; Captain, 6th July, 1855; served Crimean Campaign, 1855 (present at the fall of Sebastopol); transferred to 84th Regiment of Foot, 8th January, 1856; served Indian Mutiny, 1857-58 (present at the siege and capture of Delhi, attached to the 9th Lancers, Bolundshuhar, 2nd relief of Lucknow and Secundra Bagh, assault and capture of Lucknow, Koolsie and Baree); wounded at Delhi and Secundra Bagh; transferred to 10th Light Dragoons, 24th August, 1858; transferred to 7th Light Dragoons, 7th December, 1858; Brevet Major, 28th May, 1859; served with Indian forces in China, 1860 (present at the capture of Peking, storming of the Northern Taku Forts); ADC to General Sir Hope Grant in China, 1860; unattached, 5th February, 1861; Major, 15th February, 1861; Brevet Lieutenant Colonel, 20th July, 1870; Lieutenant Colonel, 23rd July, 1870; retired 31st July, 1873; Major, London Scottish Volunteers until shortly before his death.

Rewards, Decorations and Medals: Victoria Cross (for action at Bolundshuhur, India, 28th September, 1857); Crimea Medal (clasp for Sebastopol); Indian Mutiny Medal (clasps for Delhi, Relief of Lucknow and Lucknow); China Medal (clasps for Taku Forts 1860 and Pekin 1860); M. in D. (Indian Mutiny, 14 times); Turkish Crimea Medal; Turkish Order of the Medjidie, 5th Class.

Post-Service Employment: Member of Parliament for Lichfield, 1859-68 and Bewdley, 1869-74.

Married: Amelia Maria, daughter of Rev. Thomas Ligh Claughton, Bishop of Rochester, 1st December, 1863. After Anson's death, she married the 8th Duke of Argyll.

Children: None.

Died: Cannes, France, 17th November, 1877. He was living in the South of France due to ill health.

Buried: Cimitière Protestant du Grand Jas, Avenue de Grasse, Cannes, France.

Memorials: Cimitière Protestant du Grand Jas, Cannes, France; Lichfield Cathedral, Staffordshire. Anson Memorial Sword presented to the cadet obtaining the highest mark in the written examination at RMA Sandhurst.

Location of VC: Held by the National Trust. Not on public display.

Citation for VC: L.G. 24th December, 1858.

"For conspicuous bravery at Bolundshahur on 28th September, 1857. The 9th Light Dragoons had charged through the town and were reforming on the serai, the enemy attemped to close the entrance by drawing their carts across it, so as to shut in the cavalry and form a cover from which to fire upon them. Captain Anson, taking a lance, dashed out of the gateway and knocked the drivers off their carts. Owing to a wound in his left hand received at Delhi he could not stop his horse, and rode into the middle of the enemy who fired a volley at him, one ball passing through his coat. At Lucknow, at the assault of the Secundra Bagh, on 16th November, 1857, he entered with a storming party on the gates being burst open. He had his horse killed and was himself slightly wounded. He has shown the greatest gallantry on every occasion and has slain many enemies in fight."

He was decorated with the VC by H.M. Queen Victoria at a ball held at Buckingham Palace, 8th June, 1859.

LIEUTENANT ROBERT BLAIR
2nd Dragoon Guards (Queen's Bays)

Full Name: Robert Blair.

Place of Birth: Aventoun, Linlithgow, Scotland.

Date of Birth: 13th March, 1834.

Father: William Blair.

Mother: Isabell Cornelia Blair, daughter of Colonel Charles Cragie Halkett of Lawshill, Fifeshire, Scotland.

Father's Occupation: Barrister. He later became Mr. Justice Blair of Corfu (his father was Lord President Blair, senior Scottish officer of the law).

Education: Early education not known. Read law at Balliol College, Oxford.

Service Record: Cornet, 9th Queen's Royal Lancers, 16th December, 1853 (by purchase); Lieutenant, 2nd November, 1855 (by purchase); exchanged, 2nd Dragoon Guards, 20th December, 1856; Captain, 1858; served Indian Mutiny, 1857-58 (present at the assault on Delhi where his horse was killed under him).

Rewards, Decorations and Medals: Victoria Cross (for action at Bolundshuhur, India, 28th September, 1857); Indian Mutiny Medal (clasps for Lucknow and Delhi).

Married: Not married.

Died: Cawnpore, India, 28th March, 1859.

Buried: —

Location of VC: Queen's Dragoon Guards Museum, Shrewsbury.

Citation for VC: L.G. 18th June, 1858.
"A most gallant feat was here performed by Lieutenant Blair, who was ordered to take a party of one serjeant (sic) and twelve men and bring in a deserted ammunition wagon. As his party approached, a body of fifty or sixty of the enemy's horse came down upon him, from a village, where they had remained unobserved; without a moment's hestitation he formed up his men, and, regardless of the odds, gallantly led them on, dashing through the rebels. He made good his retreat without losing a man, leaving nine of them dead on the field. Of these he killed four himself; but, to my regret, after having run a native officer through the body with his sword, he was severely wounded, the joint of his shoulder being nearly severed."

He was decorated with the VC by H.M. Queen Victoria on Southsea Common, Hampshire, 3rd August, 1858. (The citation was taken from Major-General Sir James Hope Grant's despatch of 10th January, 1858).

N.B. When the VC was established, Blair and Lt. A. S. Jones, decided to do everything possible to win the award. Both achieved their ambition. Blair was the cousin of James Blair, VC.

LIEUTENANT THOMAS HACKETT
23rd Regiment of Foot

Full Name: Thomas Bernard Hackett.

Place of Birth: Not known. The family resided at Moor Park, King's County, Ireland and Riverstown, County Tipperary, Ireland.

Date of Birth: 15th June, 1836.

Father: Thomas Hackett.

Mother: Jane Hackett (daughter of Mr. Bernard Shaw of Monktown Castle, Co. Cork, Ireland).

Father's Occupation: Landowner, High Sheriff for King's County, 1844.

Education: –

Service Record: Commissioned Ensign, 6th Regiment of Foot, 7th June, 1854 (by purchase); transferred to 23rd Regiment of Foot (Royal Welch Fusiliers), 3rd November, 1854; Lieutenant, 9th February, 1855; served Crimean Campaign (present during the siege and fall of Sebastopol); served Indian Mutiny, 1857-58 (present during the relief and capture of Lucknow); Captain, 26th January, 1858 (by purchase); Major, 3rd September, 1870; Brevet Lieutenant Colonel; served Ashanti War, 1873-4 (2nd R.W.F.); Lieutenant Colonel, 1st April, 1874 on which date he retired from the army by selling his rank.

Rewards, Decorations and Medals: Victoria Cross (for action at Secundra Bagh, 18th November, 1857); Crimean Medal (clasp for Sebastopol); Indian Mutiny Medal (clasps for Relief of Lucknow and Lucknow); Ashantee Medal 1873-74; Turkish Crimea Medal.

Post-Service Employment: Landowner, Justice of the Peace, Co. Tipperary, Ireland. Resided at Arrabeg, Co. Tipperary.

Married: Josephine, daughter of Reverend Joseph Marshall of Barrone Court, Co. Tipperary, 1874.

Children: None recorded.

Died: 5th October, 1880, of gunshot wounds sustained whilst out shooting for partridge at Arrabeg, Co. Tipperary. An inquest returned a verdict of accidental death.

Buried: 8th October, 1880, Marshall Family Vault, Lockeen Churchyard, Borrisokane, Co. Tipperary.

Memorials: –

Location of the VC: Not known.

Citation for VC: L.G. 12th April, 1859.

"For daring gallantry at Secundra Baugh, Lucknow, on the 18th November, 1857, in having, with others, rescued a Corporal of the 23rd Regiment who was lying wounded and exposed to a very heavy fire. Also for conspicuous bravery in having, under a heavy fire, ascended the roof and cut the thatch of a Bungalow to prevent its being set on fire. This was a most important service at the time."

He is believed to have been decorated with the VC by Lord Clyde at Lucknow, India.

PRIVATE GEORGE MONGER
23rd Regiment of Foot

Full Name: George Monger.

Place of Birth: Woodmancote, Basingstoke, Hampshire.

Date of Birth: 3rd March, 1840.

Father: Joseph Monger.

Mother: Jane Monger (nee Carnmie).

Father's Occupation: Labourer.

Education: Not known.

Pre-Service Employment: Labourer.

Service Record: Enlisted 23rd Regiment of Foot, Royal Welch Fusiliers, at Winchester, 10th November, 1855 (Service No. 5202) as a Boy Soldier; served Indian Mutiny 1857-58 (present at relief and capture of Lucknow) as a Drummer; discharged at Walmer, 9th November, 1868 (his intention being to reside at North Walton, Hampshire).

Rewards, Decorations and Medals: Victoria Cross (for action at the Secundra Bagh, Lucknow, 18th November, 1857); Indian Mutiny Medal (clasps for relief of Lucknow and Lucknow).

Post Service Employment: Builder's labourer and bricklayer.

Married: Mary Ann Love at Basingstoke, Hampshire, December, 1869.

Children: Five (four others died at birth or shortly afterwards).

Died: 9th August, 1887, of consumption, at his home, 25 Tower Road, St. Leonards on Sea, Sussex. Monger had suffered from this illness for over a year and had pawned his VC and medal. When Major General Sherer heard of the family's poverty he wrote to the Hastings Observer and, as a consequence, the Duke of Cambridge arranged for payments to be made to them from the Woodman's Trust. In addition the local population of Hastings donated £120 to the family shortly before Monger's death. His son was educated at the Duke of York's School. As Monger had spent over three years in Boy Service he was only entitled to a pension for just under 10 years' service.

Buried: Grave Space E, Section H, number E.18, Hastings Borough Cemetery, 13th August, 1887. This was a Common Grave, but in 1889 it was purchased by a local resident and a headstone was erected.

Memorials: Borough Cemetery, Hastings; St. James' Church, Woodmancote, Hampshire.

Location of VC: RWF Museum, Caernarfon Castle, Caernarfon.

Citation for VC: L.G. 12th April, 1859.

"Private George Monger volunteered to accompany Lieutenant Hackett when he assisted in bringing in a corporal of the 23rd Regiment."

He is believed to have been decorated with the VC by Lord Clyde at Lucknow, India.

N.B. See entry for Lieutenant Thomas Hackett for details.

TRUMPETER THOMAS MONAGHAN
2nd Dragoon Guards (Queen's Bays)

Full Name: Thomas Monaghan.

Place of Birth: Abergavenny, Monmouthshire.

Date of Birth: 18th October, 1833.

Father: Thomas Monaghan.

Mother: Frances Monaghan (nee McAdam).

Father's Occupation: Soldier (8th Hussars).

Education: No school certificate but he was able to sign his name well on enlistment.

Service Record: Attested 3rd Light Dragoons at Westminster, 6th July, 1847 (his age being incorrectly given as 14 years and 3 months) (Service No. 1158); Trumpeter, 6th March, 1851; served in the Indian Mutiny (present at Lucknow) 1857-58; served for eleven months with the Osmandi Irregular Cavalry; re-engaged in India, 10th March, 1863; reduced to Private (date not known); Trumpeter, 7th July, 1868; reduced to Private, 28th June, 1870; Private, 29th November, 1871; discharged at Woolwich, 10th May, 1873; served with the 3rd Kent Position Artillery Band.

Rewards, Decorations and Medals: Victoria Cross (for action at Jamo, near Sundeela Oudh, India, 8th October, 1858); Indian Mutiny Medal (clasp for Lucknow).

Post-Service Employment: Army Pensioner. Trade recorded on discharge papers as Groom. He resided at 38, Ogilby Street, Woolwich, c. 1875.

Married: Margaret, c. 1870.

Children: None recorded.

Died: 10th November, 1895, at his home, 1 Pellipar Road, Woolwich.

Buried: 16th November, 1895, Section 33 (Roman Catholic), Plot 826, Woolwich Cemetery.

Memorials: Although buried in a private plot no marker was erected by his family. In 1967, a headstone was placed on his grave by the Queen's Dragoon Guards Old Comrades Association.

Location of VC: Queen's Dragoon Guards Regimental Museum, Shrewsbury.

Citation for VC: L.G. 11th November, 1862.
"For saving the life of Lieutenant Colonel Seymour, CB, commanding the regiment, in an attack made on him on 8th October, 1858, by mutinous sepoys, in a dense jungle of sugar canes from which an attempt was made to dislodge them. The mutineers were between 30 and 40 in number. They suddenly opened fire on Lieutenant Colonel Seymour and his party at a few yards' distance, and immediately rushed in upon them with drawn (native) swords. Pistolling a man, cutting at him and emptying with deadly effect at arm's length every barrel of his revolver, Lieutenant Colonel Seymour was cut down by two sword cuts when the two men above recommended rushed to his rescue, and the Trumpeter shooting a man with his pistol in the act of cutting at him and both Trumpeter and Dragoon driving at the enemy with their swords, enabled him to rise and assist in defending himself again, when the whole of the enemy were despatched. The occurrence took place soon after the action near Sundeela Oudh on the date above mentioned."

He is believed to have been decorated with the VC by General Sir Hugh Rose, G.O.C. India, at Benares, 1863.

N.B. The Dragoon mentioned in the citation was Private Charles Anderson, VC.

PRIVATE CHARLES ANDERSON
2nd Dragoon Guards (Queen's Bays)

Full Name: Charles Anderson.

Place of Birth: Liverpool.

Date of Birth: Circa 1827.

Father: —

Mother: —

Father's Occupation: —

Education: —

Pre-Service Employment: —

Service Record: Enlisted in 2nd Dragoon Guards at Dublin, 11th December, 1845 (Service No. 875); promoted to Corporal, circa 1858 (field promotion for gallantry); twice demoted from Corporal; served Indian Mutiny, 1857-8; discharged as a Corporal at Colchester. at his own request, 28th June, 1870 (his intended place of residence was given as Dublin).

Rewards, Decorations and Medals: Victoria Cross (for action at Jamo, near Sundeela Oudh, India, 8th October, 1858); Indian Mutiny Medal (clasp for Lucknow); received 5 Good Conduct Badges.

Post-Service Employment: Details not known but he could have been a coal miner (see details of his death below).

Married: No record of marriage.

Children: —

Died: The details of his death are not known. A Charles Anderson, coal miner, died from a fractured skull after falling off the cliffs at Seaham Harbour, Sunderland, on 19th April, 1899, but there is no evidence to suggest that this man and Anderson, VC, were the same person, other than the fact that the miner's age at the time of his death indicated that he was born at about the same time as Anderson, VC. The last entry in the Army Pension Records shows a payment being made to Anderson, VC, at Dublin in 1877. There are no records of Anderson's death in that city at that time or in the years following.

Buried: No details available. The Charles Anderson that died in Sunderland (who resided as a lodger at Swinbank Cottages, Seaham Harbour) is not recorded as having been buried locally.

Memorials: None known.

Location of VC: Queen's Dragoon Guards Museum, Shrewsbury. For many years the regiment held what was believed to be Anderson's VC but this was found to be a copy and the genuine decoration has since been obtained by the museum.

Citation for VC: L.G. 11th November, 1862.
This was a shared citation with Trumpeter Thomas Monaghan. See Trumpeter Thomas Monaghan for details.
He is believed to have been decorated with the VC by General Sir Hugh Rose, G.O.C. India, at Benares, India, in March, 1863.

ASSISTANT SURGEON CAMPBELL DOUGLAS
2/24th Regiment of Foot

Full Name: Campbell Mellis Douglas.

Place of Birth: Grosse Isle, Quebec, Canada.

Date of Birth: 5th August, 1840.

Father: Dr. George Mellis Douglas, MD.

Mother: Charlotte Saxton Douglas, daughter of Archibald Campbell, Queen's Notary, of Quebec, Canada.

Father's Occupation: Superintendent of Grosse Isle Quarantine Station, Quebec (1836-64).

Education: St. John's College; Laval University, Quebec, Canada; Edinburgh University (MD 1861, LRCS).

Service Record: Probationary Assistant Surgeon, Nova Scotia, 1st October, 1862; Assistant Surgeon, attached 24th Regiment of Foot, Mauritius, 22nd May, 1863; Medical Officer with the Andaman Islands Expedition, 1867; transferred Royal Artillery, Nova Scotia, 31st August, 1872; Surgeon Major, 28th April, 1876; retired, 1st October, 1882; Hon. Brigade Surgeon with the rank of Surgeon Lieutenant Colonel; served as Medical Officer in Charge of the Field Hospital for 2nd Riel Expedition, Canada, 1885 (during this expedition he made an epic 200 mile journey, by canoe, through hostile territory carrying despatches).

Rewards, Decorations and Medals: Victoria Cross (for action in the Andaman Islands, Indian Ocean, 7th May, 1867); North West Canada Medal, 1885 (no clasp); Silver Medal of the Royal Humane Society (for action in the Andaman Islands, Indian Ocean, 7th May, 1867).

Post-Service Employment: Private practice at Lakefield, Ontario, Canada. He later returned to Britain where he resided at Dunmore, Essex. He was appointed Depot Medical Officer at Berwick on Tweed and retired in 1897. Financial problems resulted in his appointment as Depot Medical Officer at Perth, a position which he held until his final retirement in 1902. He wrote several books on medical subjects and also on canoeing. As a canoeist he achieved a number of remarkable journeys in a twelve-foot Canadian canoe including a single-handed crossing of the English Channel in June, 1895, and a single-handed voyage from New York to Boston in 1889. He also patented a modification to a folding boat which was later put into general use.

Married: Eleanor McMaster, widow of Valentine McMaster, VC, MD, daughter of Colonel Burmeister, RE, at Halifax, Canada, 10th August, 1874.

Children: Three sons and one daughter. His wife also had two children by her first marriage.

Died: 31st December, 1909, at his daughter's home, Birdwood, Horrington, near Wells, Somerset.

Buried: —

Location of VC: Camp Borden Military Museum, Ontario, Canada.

Citation for VC: L.G. 17th December, 1867.

"For the very gallant and daring manner in which, on 7th May, 1867, they risked their lives in manning a boat and proceeding through dangerous surf to the rescue of some of their comrades who formed part of an expedition which had been sent to the island of Little Andaman by the order of the Chief Commissioner of British Burmah, with the view of ascertaining the fate of the commander and seven of the crew of the ship ASSAM VALLEY, who had landed there and were supposed to have been murdered by the natives.

"The officer who commanded the troops on the occasion reports, 'About an hour later in the day, Dr. Douglas, 2nd Battn. 24th Reg., and the four privates referred to, gallantly manned the second gig, made their way through the surf almost to the shore but finding their boat was half filled with water they retired. A second attempt made by Dr. Douglas and party proved successful, five of us being safely passed through the surf to the boats outside. A third and last trip got the whole of the party left on shore safe to the boats.' It is stated that Dr. Douglas accomplished these trips through surf to the shore by no ordinary exertion. He stood in the bows of the boat and worked her in an intrepid and seamanlike manner, cool to a degree, as if what he was doing was an ordinary act of everyday life. The four privates behaved in an equally cool and collected manner, rowing through the roughest surf when the slightest hesitation or want of pluck on the part of any one of them would have been attended by the gravest results. It is reported that seventeen officers and men were thus saved from what might have been a fearful risk, if not certainty, of death."

This was a shared citation with Privates Bell, Murphy, Griffiths and Cooper.

He was decorated with the VC by Major-General Faunce, GOC Pegu Division, at Rangoon, Burma, 16th April, 1868.

N.B. There are two further points of interest regarding these VC awards. Very often these five VCs are cited as examples of awards that should not have been made as the act of gallantry was not in the face of the enemy. From the citation, this would appear to be the case but further investigation shows a startling omission in the report. As the party to be rescued made their way along the beach towards the boat, they came under attack from the natives. It was generally believed that the Andaman Islanders were cannibals and indeed, only a few minutes previously, the search party had come across the skulls and bodies of some of the crew of the Assam Valley. The natives fired arrows at the soldiers throughout the period of the rescue. One mistake by Douglas and his crew would certainly have resulted in death for all concerned. Douglas was already an accomplished boatman when he went to the Andaman Islands. Shortly before the VC action, he had prepared a boat for entry into a regatta in Burma. The crew which he trained was so strong that, after winning the first race, the boat was excluded from further competition in order that other boats might have a chance. The names of the crewmen of this boat have not been recorded but it is possible that it was the same crew as that which he led on 7th May, 1867.

PRIVATE DAVID BELL
2/24th Regiment of Foot

Full Name: David Bell.

Place of Birth: County Down, Ireland.

Date of Birth: Commonly believed to have been circa 1845 but, if he gave the correct age on his enlistment, he was born circa 1842.

Father: —

Mother: —

Father's Occupation: —

Education: –

Pre-Service Employment: –

Service Record: Enlisted 24th Regiment of Foot at Lisburn, Ireland, 19th April, 1860 (Service No. 330); served Mauritius, Rangoon and Secunderabad, 1863-73; served Andaman Islands Expedition, 1867; discharged at Warley, 26th May, 1873; one extant document indicates that Bell may have been promoted to Sergeant but there is no firm evidence to substantiate this.

Rewards, Decorations and Medals: Victoria Cross (for action in the Andaman Islands, Indian Ocean, 7th May, 1867).

Post-Service Employment: Employed at a cement factory as a labourer. He was later employed as a skilled labourer at No. 8 Machine Shop, Chatham Dockyard, Kent.

Married: Ann (further details not known).

Children: None recorded.

Died: 7th March, 1920, at his home 2 Unity Cottages, Gardiner Street, Gillingham, Kent.

Buried: 12th March, 1920, Grave CH782, Woodlands Cemetery, Gillingham, Kent.

Memorials: Woodlands Cemetery, Gillingham, Kent.

Location of VC: SWB Museum, Brecon.

Citation for VC: L.G. 17th December, 1867.
This was a shared citation with Asst. Surgeon Douglas and Privates Cooper, Murphy and Griffiths. See entry for Asst. Surgeon Douglas for details.

He was decorated with the VC by Major-General Faunce, GOC Pegu Division, at Rangoon, Burma, 16th April, 1868.

PRIVATE JAMES COOPER
2nd/24th Regiment of Foot

Full Name: James Cooper.

Place of Birth: Birmingham.

Date of Birth: Circa 1840, September.

Father: William Cooper.

Mother: Elizabeth Cooper, employed as a Stay Maker.

Father's Occupation: Jeweller.

Education: Illiterate (unable to sign his name on Attestation Papers).

Pre-Service Employment: Jeweller.

Service Record: Attested at Birmingham, 12th November, 1858 (Service No. 496); served overseas Mauritius and Burma; discharged at Sheffield, 31st December, 1868; recalled to Army Service, 2nd/6th Regiment of Foot, 13th April, 1878; transferred to Army Reserve, 1st August, 1878; discharged from the Army Reserve, 14th May, 1881.

Rewards, Decorations and Medals: Victoria Cross (for action at Little Andaman Island, 7th May, 1867); Two Good Conduct Badges.

Post-Service Employment: Jeweller. In 1871 he resided at Aston's Buildings, Wheeler Street, Birmingham. In 1876 his address was Back Court, 4 New John Street, Birmingham.

Married: Maria Hampton, daughter of George Hampton, market gardener, at St. Silas Church, Birmingham, 19th November, 1871. His address at this date is given as Berners Street, Birmingham.

Children: None recorded.

Died: 9th October, 1882, at his home, 43 Court Farm Street, Birmingham.

Buried: Warstone Lane Cemetery, Warstone, Hockley, Birmingham. Grave No. 1428.

Memorials: —

Location of VC: Not known.

Citation for VC: L.G. 17th December, 1867.
This was a shared citation with Asst. Surgeon Douglas and Privates Bell, Murphy and Griffiths. See entry for Asst. Surgeon Douglas for full details.
He was decorated with the VC by Major General Faunce, GOC Pegu Division, Rangoon, Burma, 16th April, 1868.

PRIVATE THOMAS MURPHY
2nd/24th Regiment of Foot

Full Name: Thomas Murphy.

Place of Birth: Dublin, Ireland.

Date of Birth: Circa 1839.

Father: —

Mother: —

Father's Occupation: —

Education: —

Pre-Service Employment: Cloth Dresser.

Service Record: Enlisted 24th Regiment at Leeds, Yorkshire, 25th April, 1859 (Service No. 1052); served Mauritius and Burma; discharged, time-expired, at Preston, 17th November, 1869.

Rewards, Decorations and Medals: Victoria Cross (for action at Little Andaman Island, 7th May, 1867).

Married: —

Children: —

Post-Service Employment: —

Died: Philadelphia, USA, 22nd March, 1900.

Buried: —

Memorials: —

Location of VC: Not known.

Citation for VC: L.G. 17th December, 1867.
This was a shared citation with Asst. Surgeon Douglas and Privates Bell, Cooper and Griffiths. See entry for Asst. Surgeon Douglas for full details.
He was decorated with the VC by Major General Faunce, GOC Pegu Division, Rangoon, Burma, 16th April, 1868.

PRIVATE WILLIAM GRIFFITHS
2nd/24th Regiment of Foot

Full Name: William Griffiths.

Place of Birth: County Roscommon, Ireland.

Date of Birth: Circa 1841.

Father: —

Mother: —

Father's Occupation: —

Education: —

Pre-Service Occupation: Collier.

Service Record: Enlisted 24th Regiment of Foot at Warwick, 11th April 1859 (Service No. 1056); served Mauritius and Burma; served Cape of Good Hope and Natal, 1st October, 1877-January, 1879; served Zululand, January, 1879.

Rewards, Decorations and Medals: Victoria Cross (for action at Little Andaman Island, 7th May, 1867); South Africa Medal (clasp for 1877-8-9).

Married: No record of any marriage.

Children: None recorded.

Died: Isandlwana, Zululand, 22nd January, 1879.

Buried: Mass grave on the battlefield at Isandlwana, June, 1879.

Memorials: Regimental Memorial, Isandlwana, Zululand.

Location of VC: SWB Museum, Brecon.

Citation for VC: L.G. 17th December, 1867.

This was a shared citation with Asst. Surgeon Douglas and Privates Bell, Cooper and Murphy. See entry for Asst. Surgeon Douglas for full details.

He was decorated with the VC by Major General Faunce, GOC Pegu Division, Rangoon, Burma, 16th April, 1868.

LIEUTENANT LORD GIFFORD
2nd/24th Regiment of Foot

Full Name: Edric Fredrick Gifford, 3rd Baron Gifford.

Place of Birth: Ampney Park, near Cirencester, Gloucestershire.

Date of Birth: 5th July, 1849.

Father: Robert Francis Gifford, 2nd Baron Gifford.

Mother: Lady Frederica Charlotte Fitzhardinge Gifford, daughter of Admiral Sir Maurice Fitzhardinge, 1st Baron Fitzhardinge, Member of Parliament for Gloucester.

Father's Occupation: Peer of the Realm and landowner.

Education: Harrow School, April, 1863-July, 1867.

Service Record: Commissioned as Ensign, 83rd Regiment of Foot, 17th April, 1869; Lieutenant, 30th November, 1872; transferred to 24th Regiment of Foot, 26th February, 1873; Captain, 1st April, 1874 (half-pay); ADC to GOC Ashanti, 8th February, 1874-4th March, 1874; Special Service Officer Ashanti War, 1873-4 (present at repulse of Ashanti Army at Abrakrampa, November, 1873, OC Scouting Party from Prah to Kumasi, led attack on Adubiassie and Amoaful, captured Ashanti advanced post at Egginasii, led attack on Becquah (slightly wounded), present at actions between Adwabin and Ordah River, battle of Ordahsu and capture of Kumasi); transferred to 1st Middlesex Regiment, 31st May, 1876; ADC to GOC Natal, 22nd February, 1875-20th October, 1875; ADC to High Commissioner for Cyprus, 10th August, 1878-11th January, 1879; served Zulu War 1879 with the 57th Regiment of Foot (afterwards Mounted Infantry) (present at the capture of the Zulu King, Cetewayo); ADC to Sir Garnet Wolseley, High Commissioner of Natal and GOC South Africa, 7th July, 1879-May, 1880; Brevet Major, 1880; Major, 24th July, 1880; retired, 1882.

Rewards, Decorations and Medals: Victoria Cross (for action during the Ashanti War, 1873-74, particularly at Becquah); Ashantee War Medal (clasp for Coomassie); South Africa Medal (clasp for 1879); M. in D. (Ashanti and Zulu Wars).

Post-Service Employment: Accepted the post of Colonial Secretary for Ceylon, April, 1880, then offered, and accepted the post of Inspector General of Police, Mauritius; Colonial Secretary for Western Australia & Senior Member of Legislative Council, 1880-83; Colonial Secretary for Gibraltar, 1883-88; Director of Chartered British South Africa Company, 1889 onwards.

Married: Sophie Catherine, daughter of General John Alfred Street, CB, 1880. She was an Hon. Serving Sister of the Order of St. John of Jerusalem. She served with the Army Nursing Service in South Africa, 1900-02.

Children: None.

Died: 5th June, 1911, at his home, Old Park, Chichester, Sussex.

Buried: 8th June, 1911, at Bosham, Sussex.

Memorials: Speech Room, Harrow School; Bosham Parish Church, Sussex.

Location of VC: Private collection.

Citation for VC: L.G. 31st March, 1874.

"For his gallant conduct during the operations and especially at the taking of Becquah. The Officer Commanding the Expeditionary Force reports that Lord Gifford was in charge of Scouts after the army crossed the Prah and it is no exaggeration to say that since the Adansi Hills were passed he daily carried his life in his hand in performance of his most dangerous duties. He hung upon the rear of the enemy, discovering their position and ferreting out their intentions. With no other white man with him he captured numerous prisoners; but Sir Garnet Wolseley brings him forward for this mark of Royal favour most especially for his conduct at the taking of Becquah, into which place he penetrated with his scouts before the troops carried it, when his gallantry and courage were most conspicuous."

He was decorated with the VC by H.M. Queen Victoria at the Windsor Park Review, 30th March, 1874.

N.B. Lord Gifford was the uncle of Captain J. F. P. Butler, who received the VC for his gallantry in the Cameroons, West Africa, in 1914.

LIEUTENANT TEIGNMOUTH MELVILL
1st/24th Regiment of Foot

Full Name: Teignmouth Melvill.

Place of Birth: 4, Clarendon Place, London.

Date of Birth: 8th September, 1842.

Father: Philip Melvill.

Mother: Elizabeth Melvill, daughter of Colonel Sandys of Lenarth, Helston, Cornwall.

Father's Occupation: Secretary to the Military Department of the East India Company.

Education: Harrow School, January, 1856-March, 1858; Cheltenham School; Trinity College, Cambridge (BA, February, 1865).

Service Record: Commissioned Ensign, 1st/24th Regiment of Foot, 20th October, 1865 (by purchase); Lieutenant, 2nd December, 1868 (by purchase); Adjutant, 7th March, 1873; served Cape Colony, 1875-77; passed entrance examination for the Staff College, 1877; returned to England to attend Staff College, January, 1878; returned to his regiment to serve in the Galeka War, February, 1878; served Zulu War, January, 1879, with Headquarters Column (present at attack on Sirayo's Stadt, 13th January, 1879, and Battle of Isandlwana, 22nd January, 1879).

Rewards, Decorations and Medals: Victoria Cross (for action following the Battle of Isandlwana, 22nd January, 1879); South Africa Medal (clasp for 1877-8-9).

Married: Sarah Elizabeth, daughter of George Thomas Reed, Esq., of Port Elizabeth, South Africa, in February, 1876.

Children: Two sons.

Died: K. in A. at the Buffalo River, Natal, 22nd January, 1879.

Buried: Isolated grave (with Lt. Coghill, VC), Buffalo River, near Fugitives Drift, Natal, 4th February, 1879.

Memorials: Buffalo River, Natal; Harrow School Chapel; Big Classical, Cheltenham School; St. Winnow's Parish Church, Cornwall; Colour Pole, 24th Regiment of Foot.

Location of VC: SWB Museum, Brecon.

Citation for VC: L.G. 2nd May, 1879.

"Memorandum. Lieutenant Melvill, of the 1st Battalion, 24th Foot, on account of the gallant efforts made by him to save the Queen's Colour of his regiment after the disaster at Isandhlwana; and also Lieutenant Coghill, 1st Battalion, 24th Foot, on account of his heroic conduct in endeavouring to save his brother officer's life, would have been recommended to Her Majesty for the Victoria Cross had they survived."

The award of the first posthumous VCs during the Boer War prompted the request that the award should be made retrospectively to Melvill and Coghill. The request was finally approved by H.M. King Edward VII and gazetted on 15th January, 1907.

The VC was sent to Lieutenant Melvill's widow in June, 1907.

N.B. For full details of this VC action see entry for Lieutenant Coghill.

LIEUTENANT NEVILL COGHILL
1st/24th Regiment of Foot

Full Name: Nevill Joseph Aylmer Coghill.

Place of Birth: Drumcondra, County Dublin, Ireland. The family also lived at Castle Townshend, County Cork, Ireland, 3 Royal Marine Terrace, Bray, County Dublin, Ireland and 21 Bolton Studios, Redcliffe Road, London.

Date of Birth: 25th January, 1852.

Father: Sir Joscelyn Coghill, Bart., J.P.

Mother: Katherine Frances Coghill, daughter of Lord Plunket.

Father's Occupation: Landowner.

Education: Haileybury College, 1865-69; RMA Sandhurst, 2nd February, 1874-April, 1874.

Service Record: Commissioned as Supernumerary Lieutenant Dublin County Militia, 13th May, 1871; commissioned Sub-Lieutenant, 24th Regiment of Foot, 26th February, 1873; Lieutenant, 13th August, 1875; served Cape Colony, 1877-8 as ADC to General Sir Arthur Cunyngham in the Galeka War; returned to England, 1878; returned to Cape Colony, 1879, as ADC to Sir Bartle Frere; granted six weeks leave to take part, with his regiment, in the invasion of Zululand, January, 1879; ADC with Colonel Glyn's Column but, due to an injured leg, he was unable to accompany that officer when he later left the camp at Isandlwana, 22nd January, 1879; present at the Battle of Isandlwana, 22nd January, 1879.

Rewards, Decorations and Medals: Victoria Cross (for action following the Battle of Isandlwana, 22nd January, 1879); South Africa Medal (clasp for 1877-8-9); M. in D. for Galeka War, 1877 and Zulu War, 1879.

Married: Not married.

Children: None.

Died: K. in A. at the Buffalo River, Natal, 22nd January, 1879.

Buried: Isolated grave (with Lt. Teignmouth Melvill, VC), Buffalo River, near Fugitives Drift, Natal, 4th February, 1879.

Memorials: Buffalo River, Natal; painting in the Chapel at Haileybury College; Colour Pole, 24th Regiment of Foot.

Location of VC: SWB Museum, Brecon.

Citation for VC: L.G. 2nd May, 1879.

This citation was shared with Lieutenant Teignmouth Melvill. See entry for Lieutenant Melvill for details.

The VC was sent to Sir E. B. Coghill, Bart., Lieutenant Coghill's brother, in February, 1907.

As the citation is somewhat obscure, it may be of value to provide full details here. When Colonel Pulleine (OC 1st/24th Regiment of Foot at Isandlwana, 22nd January, 1879) realised that the position of the British camp, which was under attack by the main Zulu force, was a hopeless one, he ordered Lieutenant Melvill to attempt to save the Queen's Colour of the battalion. As Melvill rode off, with the cased colour across his saddle, he was joined by Lieutenant Coghill and both men were pursued by Zulu warriors. They managed to reach the Buffalo River (the Natal/Zululand frontier) safely but found difficulty crossing the swollen river. Coghill managed to get across but Melvill, carrying the colour, lost his horse and was forced to hold on to a rock in the middle of the river. As soon as he saw his comrade's predicament, Lt. Coghill plunged back into the water and assisted Melvill to the Natal shore. Unfortunately, the colour was washed away downstream. The following Zulus crossed the river and caught up with the two men and after a short but gallant struggle, both were killed. Their bodies were discovered on 4th February, 1879, and they were buried where they had fallen. A small stone cairn and cross were erected to mark the spot. The Queen's Colour of the 1st/24th Regiment of Foot was subsequently recovered further down the river.

LIEUTENANT GONVILLE BROMHEAD
2nd/24th Regiment of Foot

Full Name: Gonville Bromhead.

Place of Birth: Versailles, France. The family home was at Thurlby Hall, Newark, Lincolnshire.

Date of Birth: 29th August, 1845.

Father: Sir Edmund de Gonville Bromhead, Bart.

Mother: Judith Christine Cahill Bromhead, daughter of James Wood of Woodville, Co. Sligo, Ireland.

Father's Occupation: Retired Major, Landowner.

Education: Magnus Grammar School, Newark-on-Trent.

Service Record: Commissioned Ensign 2nd/24th Regiment of Foot, 20th April, 1867 (by purchase); Lieutenant, 28th October, 1871; served in Cape Colony, 1878 and Zululand, 1879 (present at the defence of Rorke's Drift, 22nd/23rd January, 1879); Captain and Brevet Major, 23rd January, 1879; Major, 4th April, 1883; served East Indies, 1880-1882; School of Musketry, Hythe, 1882 (First Class Extra Certificate); served in Burma, 1886-88.

Rewards, Decorations and Medals: Victoria Cross (for action at Rorke's Drift, Natal, 22nd/23rd January, 1879); South Africa Medal (clasp for 1877-8-9); Burma Medal (clasps for 1885-7 and 1887-9); Brevet Major (for action at Rorke's Drift, Natal, 22nd/23rd January, 1879); M. in D. (Natal, 1879); Sword of Honour from the City of Lincoln; presented with a revolver by the tenants of Thurlby Hall.

Married: Not married.

Children: None.

Died: 9th February, 1891, at Camp Dabhaura, Allahabad, India (of Enteric Fever).

Buried: Allahabad, India.

Memorials: Magnus Grammar School, Newark-on-Trent (his portrait hangs in School House along with his uniform); Colour Pole 24th Regiment of Foot.

Location of VC: SWB Museum, Brecon.

Citation for VC: L.G. 2nd May, 1879.
"For their (Bromhead and Lt.M. Chard who commanded the defenders at Rorke's Drift) gallant conduct at the defence of Rorke's Drift, on the occasion of the attack by the Zulus on the 22nd and 23rd January, 1879.
"The Lieutenant-General Commanding the troops reports that, had it not been for the fine example and excellent behaviour of these two Officers, under the most trying circumstances, the defence of Rorke's Drift post would not have been conducted with that intelligence and tenacity which so essentially characterised it.
"The Lieutenant General adds that its success must, in a great degree, be attributable to the two young Officers who exercised the Chief Command on the occasion in question."

He was decorated with the VC by Sir Garnet Wolseley, GCMG, KCB, High Commissioner and GOC British South Africa, at Utrecht, Transvaal, 22nd August, 1879.

CORPORAL WILLIAM ALLAN
2nd/24th Regiment of Foot
Full Name: William Wilson Allan.
Place of Birth: St. Andrew's Parish, Newcastle upon Tyne, Northumberland.
Date of Birth: Circa 1844.
Father: —
Mother: —
Father's Occupation: —
Education: 2nd Class Certificate of Education.
Pre-Service Employment: —
Service Record: Attested at York, 27th October, 1859, 2nd/24th Regiment of Foot (Service No. 1240); Lance Corporal, 18th May, 1876; served as Assistant Schoolmaster, Regimental Depot, Brecon, circa 1876; Corporal, 6th July, 1877; Lance Sergeant, 22nd May, 1878; reverted to Corporal, 21st October, 1878; served Cape Colony and Natal, 1878-9 (present at the defence of Rorke's Drift, 22nd/23rd January, 1879, where he was wounded in the left shoulder and partly disabled for the remainder of his life); Provisional Lance Sergeant, 11th November, 1879, whilst serving with the 3rd/24th Regiment (Militia) at Brecon; Sergeant, 16th June, 1880; Sergeant Instructor of Musketry 4th Volunteer Battalion, South Wales Borderers.
Rewards, Decorations and Medals: Victoria Cross (for action at Rorke's Drift, Natal, 22nd/23rd January, 1879); South Africa Medal (clasp for 1877-8-9); Good Shooting and Judging Distance Prize, 1878.
Married: Sarah Ann Reeves at Brecon, 16th August, 1876.
Children: Seven children. Details not known.
Died: 12th March, 1890, at his home, 85 Monnow Street, Monmouth.
Buried: Monmouth Cemetery, Monmouth.
Memorials: Monmouth Cemetery, Monmouth.
Location of VC: SWB Museum, Brecon.
Citation for VC: L.G. 2nd May, 1879.
"It was chiefly due to the courageous conduct of these men that communication with the hospital was kept up at all. Holding together at all costs a most dangerous post, raked in reverse by the enemy's fire from the hill, they were both severely wounded, but their determined conduct enabled the patients to be withdrawn from the hospital, and when incapacitated by their wounds from fighting, they continued, as soon as their wounds had been dressed, to serve out ammunition to their comrades during the night."
This citation was shared with Private Frederick Hitch.
He was decorated with the VC by H.M. Queen Victoria at Windsor Castle, 9th December, 1879.

PRIVATE FREDERICK HITCH
2nd/24th Regiment of Foot
Full Name: Frederick Hitch.
Place of Birth: Edmonton, Middlesex.
Date of Birth: 28th November, 1856.
Father: —

Mother: —

Father's Occupation: —

Education: Unable to sign his name on the attestation papers.

Pre-Service Employment: Bricklayer's labourer.

Service Record: Attested Westminster Police Court, 7th March, 1877; Private, 2nd/24th Regiment of Foot, 9th March, 1877 (Service No. 1362); served Galeka War, Cape Colony and Natal, 1878; served Zulu War, 1879 (present at the defence of Rorke's Drift, 22nd/23rd January, 1879, severely wounded in the right shoulder by a roughly made Zulu bullet which shattered the bone and permanently disabled him); patient at Netley Hospital, 10th June, 1879-25th August, 1879; discharged as unfit for military service, Netley, 25th August, 1879.

Rewards, Decorations and Medals: Victoria Cross (for action at Rorke's Drift, Natal, 22nd/23rd January, 1879); South Africa Medal (clasp for 1877-8-9).

Post-Service Employment: His discharge papers give his proposed employment as labourer. He was, for a time, employed in the Corps of Commissionaires at the Imperial Institute, London, and later at the United Service Institute, Whitehall. He then became a London Cab Driver in which occupation he remained until his death.

Married: Emma Matilda Maurice, daughter of the Manager of the Cafe Royal, Regent Street, July, 1880.

Children: Three sons and three daughters.

Died: 7th January, 1913, at his home, 62 Cranbrook Road, Ealing, Middlesex (during a London taxi strike).

Buried: No. 17, Block P, St. Nicholas' Churchyard, Old Chiswick, London, 11th January, 1913. In addition to the family and the military representatives it was estimated that over 1,500 London cabbies attended the funeral.

Memorials: St. Nicholas' Churchyard, Old Chiswick, London.

Location of VC: His VC was stolen from his coat whilst he was a commissionaire. A replacement was produced by order of King Edward VII and he was presented with it by the king in 1908. The original is still missing. The replacement is held by the SWB Museum, Brecon.

Citation for VC: L.G. 2nd May, 1879.

This was a shared citation with Corporal William Allan. See Corporal William Allan for details.

He was decorated with the VC by H.M. Queen Victoria at Netley Hospital, 12th August, 1879.

PRIVATE WILLIAM JONES
2nd/24th Regiment of Foot

Full Name: William Jones.

Place of Birth: Generally believed to have been Evesham in Worcestershire but there is evidence that it may have been Bristol.

Date of Birth: Circa 1839.

Father: James Jones.

Mother: —

Father's Occupation: Builder's labourer.

Education: —

Pre-Service Employment: Boot Closer.

Service Record: Attested at Birmingham, 21st December, 1858, for 2nd/24th Regiment of Foot (Service No. 593); Corporal, 1st September, 1859; reduced to Private, 5th September, 1860; served Mauritius and Burma; re-engaged at Rangoon, 10th January, 1868; served India; served Cape Colony and Natal (Galeka and Zulu Wars, 1877-79, present at the defence of Rorke's Drift, 22nd/23rd January, 1879); discharged at Netley Hospital, 2nd February, 1880, due to chronic rheumatism.

Rewards, Decorations and Medals: Victoria Cross (for action at Rorke's Drift, 22nd/23rd January, 1879); South Africa Medal (clasp for 1879); Long Service and Good Conduct Medal; Three Good Conduct Badges.

Post-Service Employment: He was unable to obtain regular employment after his discharge despite an attempt to return to his trade in the boot industry. He is known to have worked in the theatre re-enacting the defence of Rorke's Drift. He also toured with Buffalo Bill's Wild West Show in the 1880s. In later life he was employed as a labourer. After discharge, he resided in Lupin Street, Birmingham, but later moved, with his second wife, to Rutland Street, Chorlton, Lancashire. In 1910 he was admitted to New Bridge Street Workhouse, Manchester, for one night, having been found wandering the streets (this was a regular occurrence as he would awake in the night believing that he was back in South Africa and that the Zulus were about to attack. He would take his small granddaughter from her bed and then leave the house in the middle of the night).

Married: 1) Elizabeth, daughter of Charles Goddard, tailor, of Aldershot, 12th May, 1875. She is believed to have accompanied him to South Africa and to have died in childbirth shortly before the outbreak of the Zulu War. (2) Elizabeth Frodsham (widow), nee Walters, at St. Augustine's Church, Newton Heath, Manchester.

Children: One daughter and one son by his second marriage. He also had five stepchildren. There is also a report that he had a son by his first marriage who was sent to relatives in Wales after his birth in South Africa (believed to have been named William).

Died: At his daughter's home, 6 Brampton Street, Ardwick, Manchester, 15th April, 1913.

Buried: Philips Park Cemetery (Bradford Ward), Manchester, 21st April, 1913. Public subscription grave, D887.

Memorials: Philips Park Cemetery, Manchester. The grave does not record that he was a VC.

Location of VC: Jones pawned the VC in his later years and was unable to redeem it. Now held by the South Wales Borderers Museum, Brecon.

Citation for VC: L.G. 2nd May, 1879.
"In another ward, facing the hill, Private William Jones and Private Robert Jones defended the post to the last, until six out of the seven patients it contained had been removed. The seventh, Sergeant Maxfield, 2nd Battalion, 24th Regiment, was delirious from fever. Although they had previously dressed him they were unable to induce him to move. When Private Robert Jones returned to endeavour to carry him away, he found him being stabbed by the Zulus as he lay in bed."
This is a shared citation with Private Robert Jones.

He was decorated with the VC by H.M. Queen Victoria at Windsor, 13th January, 1880.

PRIVATE ROBERT JONES
2nd/24th Regiment of Foot

Full Name: Robert Jones.

Place of Birth: Tynewydd, Clytha, Nr. Raglan, Monmouthshire.

Date of Birth: 19th August, 1857.

Father: —

Mother: —

Father's Occupation: Probably an agricultural labourer.

Education: 4th Class Certificate of Education.

Pre-Service Employment: Labourer.

Service Record: Attested at Monmouth, 2nd/24th Regiment of Foot, 10th January, 1876; joined the regiment 28th January, 1876 (Service No. 716); served Cape Colony and Natal, 1878-9 (present at the defence of Rorke's Drift, Natal, 22nd/23rd January, 1879); served India 1880-81; returned to Britain 25th November, 1881; transferred to the Army Reserve, 26th January, 1882; recalled for service with South Wales Borderers, 2nd August, 1882; transferred to the Army Reserve, 7th February, 1883; discharged from the Army Reserve, 26th January, 1888.

Rewards, Decorations and Medals: Victoria Cross (for action at Rorke's Drift, Natal, 22nd/23rd January, 1879); South Africa Medal (clasp for 1877-8-9).

Post-Service Employment: He was a farm labourer employed by Major De la Hay at Crossway House, Peterchurch, Herefordshire. He also owned his own smallholding at Tricodivor Farm, St. Margarets Vowchurch, Herefordshire.

Married: Elizabeth Hopkins at Llantilio, 7th January, 1885.

Children: One son and four daughters.

Died: During the summer of 1898, Robert Jones complained of headaches and suffered a form of convulsion. On 6th September, 1898, he borrowed his employer's gun, stating that he was going to go and shoot crows. A maid later found his body in the garden of his employer's house at Peterchurch. He had shot himself in the mouth. An inquest held the following day returned a verdict of suicide through unsound mind.

Buried: 8th September, 1898 at Peterchurch, Herefordshire.

Memorials: Peterchurch, Herefordshire.

Location of VC: Private Collection.

Citation for VC: L.G. 2nd May, 1879.

This citation was shared with Private William Jones. See Private William Jones for details.

He was decorated with the VC by Sir Garnet Wolseley, High Commissioner and GOC South Africa at Utrecht, Transvaal, 11th September, 1879.

PRIVATE HENRY HOOK
2nd/24th Regiment of Foot

Full Name: Alfred Henry Hook.

Place of Birth: Alney, Churcham, Gloucestershire. Later, whilst serving in the army, his address was Drybridge Street, Monmouth.

Date of Birth: 6th August, 1850.

Father: Henry Hook.

Mother: Eleanor Hook (nee Higgs).

Father's Occupation: Tenant Farmer.

Education: —

Pre-Service Employment: Farm labourer.

Service Record: Served for five years in the Monmouthshire Militia; attested at Monmouth, 13th March, 1877, and posted to 2nd/24th Regiment of Foot, 11th May, 1877 (Service No. 1373); served Cape Colony and Natal, 1878-79 (present at the defence of Rorke's Drift, 22nd/23rd January, 1879, received a scalp wound from a Zulu assagai which, in later years, caused him some discomfort); purchased his discharge, 25th June, 1880 (for £18); served for nearly twenty years in the 1st Volunteer Battalion, Royal Fusiliers; Sergeant Instructor of Musketry.

Rewards, Decorations and Medals: Victoria Cross (for action at Rorke's Drift, Natal, 22nd/23rd January, 1879); South Africa Medal (clasp for 1877-8-9); Good Conduct Badge; Marksman Badge.

Post-Service Employment: On his discharge he went to London where he resided at Sydenham Hill and was employed as a labourer at the British Museum from 26th December, 1881. He later became a cloakroom attendant at the same museum, a post which he held until ill-health forced him to retire on 31st December, 1904 (receiving a Treasury gratuity for his service). Whilst in London he also resided in Pimlico and at 33 Fitzroy Square. He was a member of the Loyal St. James Lodge of the Oddfellows. After retiring he returned to Gloucestershire.

Married: There is some mystery surrounding Hook's marriage. It is believed that he was married before enlisting in the army and that his wife bore him one daughter. This marriage is supposed to have ended when his wife received reports that he had been killed in South Africa and, when he returned, he found that she had remarried. There is no evidence to substantiate this story. He did marry Ada Letitia, daughter of William Frederick Taylor, goldsmith of the City of London, at St. Andrew's Church, Islington, 10th April, 1897.

Children: Two daughters by his marriage to Ada Taylor.

Died: 12th March, 1905, at his home, 2 Osborne Villas, Roseberry Avenue, Gloucester, of Pulmonary Consumption. His health had always been poor since his return from South Africa.

Buried: Churcham, Gloucestershire, 18th March, 1905. Amongst the mourners was Frederick Hitch, VC.

Memorials: Churcham, Gloucestershire; Brecon Cathedral, Brecon.

Location of VC: SWB Museum, Brecon.

Citation for VC: L.G. 2nd May, 1879.

This was a shared citation with Private John Williams (Fielding). See Private John Williams for details.

He was decorated with the VC by Sir Garnet Wolseley, High Commissioner and GOC South Africa, 3rd August, 1879, at Fort Melvill, Rorke's Drift, Natal. He was the only one of the Rorke's Drift VCs to be decorated at the scene of the VC action.

PRIVATE JOHN WILLIAMS
2nd/24th Regiment of Foot

Full Name: John Fielding (Williams was a pseudonym which he had adopted to prevent his parents tracing him after he had joined the army).

Place of Birth: Merthyr Road, Abergavenny, Monmouthshire. The family moved to live in Cwmbran, Monmouthshire when he was aged about 5 years.

Date of Birth: 24th May, 1857.

Father: Michael Fielding.

Mother: Margaret Fielding (nee Godsil).

Father's Occupation: Gardener.

Education: —

Pre-Service Employment: Employed aged 8 years by the Patent Nut & Bolt Works, Cwmbran.

Service Record: Enlisted in the Monmouthshire Militia, February, 1877; attested at Monmouth, 24th Regiment of Foot, 27th May, 1877 (Service No. 1395); joined 2nd/24th Regiment of Foot at Chatham, June, 1877; served Cape Colony and Natal, 1877-79 (present at the defence of Rorke's Drift, 22nd/23rd January, 1879); served India, 1880-1883; transferred to the Army Reserve, 1883; discharged from the Reserve, 22nd May, 1893; served as Sergeant 3rd Volunteer Battalion, South Wales Borderers; volunteered for service during the Great War and served with the SWB at Brecon Barracks.

Rewards, Decorations and Medals: Victoria Cross (for action at Rorke's Drift, Natal, 22nd/23rd January, 1879); South Africa Medal (clasp for 1877-8-9).

Post-Service Employment: Details not known.

Married: Elizabeth Murphy.

Children: Three sons (one KIA with the SWB during the retreat from Mons, 1914) and two daughters.

Died: 25th November, 1932 at his daughter's home, Tycoch, Cwmbran, Monmouthshire. He lived at the time with another daughter at 28 Cocker Avenue, Cwmbran. Last surviving Rorke's Drift VC.

Buried: Llanfihangel Churchyard, Llantarnam, Monmouthshire, 29th November, 1932. His coffin had laid-in-state in the Catholic Church, Wesley Street, Cwmbran, prior to the funeral.

Memorials: Llanfihangel Churchyard, Llantarnam, Monthmouthshire; John Fielding House (residential home for the mentally handicapped), Llantarnam, Monmouthshire.

Location of VC: SWB Museum, Brecon.

Citation for VC: L.G. 2nd May, 1879.

"Private John Williams was posted with Private Joseph Williams and Private William Horrigan, 1st Battalion 24th Regiment, in a distant room of the hospital, which they held for more than an hour, so long as they had a round of ammunition left; as communication was for the time cut off, the Zulus were able to advance and burst open the door; they dragged out Private Joseph Williams and two of the patients, and assegaied them. Whilst the Zulus were occupied with the slaughter of these men a lull took place, during which Private John Williams who, with two of the patients, were the only men now left alive in this ward, succeeded in knocking a hole in the partition, and in taking the two patients into the next ward, where he found Private Hook.

"These two men together, one man working whilst the other fought and held the enemy at bay with his bayonet, broke through three more partitions, and were thus enabled to bring eight patients through a small window into the inner line of defence."

This was a shared citation with Private Henry Hook.

He was decorated with the VC by Major General Anderson, GOC Gibraltar at Almeda Parade Ground, Gibraltar, 1st March, 1880.

LIEUTENANT EDWARD BROWNE
1st/24th Regiment of Foot

Full Name: Edward Stevenson Browne.

Place of Birth: Park Terrace, St. Andrew the Great, Cambridge.

Date of Birth: 23rd December, 1852.

Father: Salwey Browne.

Mother: Elizabeth Browne (nee Stevenson).

Father's Occupation: Captain, Durham Light Infantry. He was a student at Cambridge University at the time of his son's birth.

Education: — ; RMA Sandhurst, 2nd August, 1869-31st December, 1870.

Service Record: Commissioned as an Ensign, 1st/24th Regiment of Foot, 23rd September, 1871; Lieutenant, 28th October, 1871; served Malta, 1872, Gibraltar, 1872, Cape Colony, 1874-77 (expedition to Griqualand West, 1875), Natal, Transvaal and Zululand 1877-79 (OC 1st Squadron Mounted Infantry, present at battles of Kambula and Ulundi); served 2nd Campaign against Sekukuni, 1879; Captain, 19th May, 1880; Adjutant, 4th Volunteer Battalion South Wales Borderers, 19th September, 1881-18th September, 1886; Major, 2nd November, 1885; Lieutenant Colonel, 2nd South Wales Borderers, 8th April, 1893; DAAG, Musketry, Bengal, 3rd November, 1891-7th July, 1892; Colonel, 8th April, 1897; OC 24 Regimental District, Brecon, 8th April, 1897; AAG North East District, 4th March, 1900-6th September, 1902; Temporary Brigadier General, 7th September, 1902; GOC 5th Army Corps, York, 1902; Brigadier General, 6th & 11th Brigades, 2nd Army Corps, Southern Command, 10th November, 1903-9th November, 1906; retired, 10th November, 1906; Hon. Colonel West Yorkshire Regiment, 2nd Volunteer Battalion, 3rd December, 1902 until his death.

Rewards, Decorations and Medals: Victoria Cross (for action at Hlobana, Zululand, 29th March, 1879); CB (L.G. 24th June, 1904); South Africa Medal (clasp for 1878-9); Diamond Jubilee Medal (1897); M. in D. (Zulu Campaign).

Post-Service Employment: Retired General Officer.

Married: Amelia Wright, at Edinburgh, 6th November, 1879.

Children: Two sons and two daughters.

Died: Montreux, Switzerland, 16th July, 1907. His address at this time was Gun House, Portsmouth.

Buried: —

Memorials: —

Location of VC: South Wales Borderers Museum, Brecon.

Citation for VC: L.G. 17th June, 1879.

"For his gallant conduct on 29th March, 1879, when the Mounted Infantry were being driven in by the enemy at Inholbana, in galloping back and twice assisting on his horse (under heavy fire and within a few yards of the enemy) one of the mounted men who must otherwise have fallen into enemy hands."

He was decorated with the VC by Sir Garnet Wolseley, High Commissioner and GOC British South Africa, at Pine Tree Camp, Natal, August, 1879.

PRIVATE JOHN DOOGAN
1st Dragoon Guards (The King's)

Full Name: John Doogan.

Place of Birth: Augrim, County Galway, Ireland.

Date of Birth: March, 1853.

Father: —

Mother: —

Father's Occupation: —

Education: —

Pre-Service Employment: —

Service Record: Enlisted 1st Dragoon Guards, 1873 (Service No. 1401); served South Africa, 1879, during the Zulu War (present at Ulundi, ??); served Boer War, 1881 (present at Laing's Nek, 28th January, 1881, severely wounded) as Servant to Major Brownlow; discharged from the army, unfit for military service, at Netley Hospital, 1881; enlisted for service in the Great War as Recruiting Sergeant.

Rewards, Decorations and Medals: Victoria Cross (for action at Laing's Nek, South Africa, 28th January, 1881); South Africa Medal (clasp for 1879); Good Conduct Medal (for six years service). He received a private pension of £20 per annum in the will of Major Brownlow, commencing in 1902.

Post-Service Employment: Coachman; lodgeman; constable, Royal Irish Constabulary; Royal Mail van driver; licencee Black Lion Inn, Welshpool; farmer, small-holding, Welshpool. Known to have resided at Cause Mountain, Westbury, Salop and Cheriton, Folkestone, Kent.

Married: 1) Mary Evans of Montgomeryshire, 1882 (she died in 1924); 2) Maria Roberts, at Welshpool, 1928. This marriage was dissolved as she was already married; 3) Bessie, daughter of Mrs. W. Evans of Ysgyborgoch, Welshpool, 1933 (she was then aged in her twenties).

Children: Four sons and five daughters (two of his sons killed in the Great War).

Died: 5 Folly Road, Folkestone, Kent, 24th January, 1940.

Buried: Military Cemetery, Shorncliffe, Kent.

Memorials: Military Cemetery, Shorncliffe, Kent.

Location of VC: He bequeathed it to the 1st Dragoon Guards in his will. It was stolen during the VC Centenary Exhibition, 1956. Now held by a collector in USA.

Citation for VC: L.G. 14th March, 1882.

"For gallant conduct during the action of Laing's Nek on the 28th January, 1881. During the charge of the mounted men Private Doogan, servant to Major Brownlow, 1st Dragoon Guards, seeing that officer (whose horse had been shot) dismounted and among the Boers, rode up and (though himself severely wounded) dismounted and pressed Major Brownlow to take his horse, receiving another wound while trying to induce him to accept it."

He was decorated with the VC by the Superintendent of Pensions at Cork, Ireland, in May 1882. It had been intended that he should be decorated by H.M. Queen Victoria at Windsor, 13th May, 1882, but his address was not known to the authorities and he was not therefore contacted in time.

PRIVATE SAMUEL VICKERY
1st Dorset Regiment

Full Name: Samuel Vickery.

Place of Birth: Wambrook, Nr. Chard, Somerset.

Date of Birth: 6th February, 1873.

Father: Simon Vickery.

Mother: Sarah Vickery (nee Singleton).

Father's Occupation: Farm labourer.

Education: –

Pre-Service Employment: Labourer.

Service Record: Enlisted 1st Dorset Regiment, at Cardiff Barracks, 26th July, 1893 (Service No. 3937); transferred to 2nd Dorset Regiment, Belfast, 1895; transferred to 1st Dorset Regiment, Wellington, India, 1896; served Tirah Campaign 1897-98 (wounded by a severe sword cut across the foot, 16th November, 1897); invalided to Britain, 1898, treated at Netley Hospital; transferred to 2nd Dorset Regiment; served South Africa, 1899-1901; captured by Boers but escaped after four days, severely wounded at Nooitgedacht, 13th December, 1900 (present at Wittebergen, Diamond Hill, capture of Johannesburg, Driefontein, Paardeberg, Relief of Kimberley); invalided out of the army, unfit for military service, 31st August, 1901; enlisted 6th Dorset Regiment, 17th September, 1914 (Service No. 11601); served France, 1915, promoted to Corporal; declared unfit for further service in the line and transferred to PoW Camp guard, France, 1916; transferred to Labour Corps, 15th July, 1918 (Service No. 56966); discharged, 31st March, 1920.

Rewards, Decorations and Medals: Victoria Cross (for action at Dargai, Tirah, 20th October, 1897 and Warah Valley, Tirah, 16th November, 1897); India General Service Medal (clasps for Punjab Frontier, 1897-98 and Tirah, 1897-98); Queen's South Africa Medal (clasps for South Africa, 1901, Wittebergen, Diamond Hill, Johannesburg, Driefontein, Paardeberg, Relief of Kimberley); 1914-15 Star; British War Medal; Victory Medal; Coronation Medal (1937).

Post-Service Employment: Male nurse, Whitchurch Hospital, Cardiff (pre-1914); Commissionaire, GPO, Cardiff until he retired in 1946.

Married: Catherine Ann Green, seamstress, at Whitchurch Hospital, Cardiff, circa 1907.

Children: None recorded.

Died: St. David's Hospital, Cardiff, 20th June, 1952. His home address at this time was 33 Romilly Crescent, Cardiff.

Buried: Cremated at Glyntaff Crematorium, Pontypridd, 25th June, 1952.

Memorials: —

Location of VC: Dorset Military Museum, Dorchester, Dorset.

Citation for VC: L.G. 20th May, 1898.

"During the attack on the Dargai Heights on the 20th October, 1897, Private Vickery ran down the slope and rescued a wounded comrade under heavy fire, bringing him back to cover. He subsequently distinguished himself with Brigadier-General Kempster's Column in the Warran Valley, killing three of the enemy who attacked him when separated from his Company."

He was decorated with the VC by H.M. Queen Victoria at Netley Hospital, 14th May, 1898, six days before the announcement appeared in the London Gazette.

CAPTAIN NEVILL SMYTH
2nd Dragoon Guards (Queen's Bays)

Full Name: Nevill Maskelyne Smyth.

Place of Birth: 13 Victoria Street, Westminster, London.

Date of Birth: 14th August, 1868.

Father: Sir Warington Wilkinson Smyth, FRS, of Marazion, Cornwall.

Mother: Lady Anna Maria Antonia Smyth, daughter of A. S. Maskelyne of Basset Down, Wiltshire.

Father's Occupation: Civil Servant.

Education: Private school, details unknown; RMA Sandhurst.

Service Record: Commissioned, 2nd Lieutenant, 2nd Dragoon Guards, 22nd August, 1888 (he joined the regiment in India); Lieutenant, 26th April, 1895; served on the Staff during the Zhob Valley Expedition, Afghan Frontier, 1890; Special Service Officer, Egypt, 24th March, 1896-8th October, 1896; served with the Egyptian Army, 9th October, 1896-8th January, 1902; Captain, 8th December, 1897; served with the Dongola Expedition, Sudan, 1896, as Orderly Officer to the OC Mounted Forces (present at the Battle of Firket and the pursuit of Suarda); Staff Officer to the Chief of Staff at Battle of Hafir and Occupation of Dongola; Staff Officer, Camel Corps; served Sudan Campaign, 1897, as Staff Officer to OC Dongola Province; DAAG and OC advanced posts at Atbara; OC Infantry and Machine Guns at bombardment of Metemmeh; served aboard Commander Beatty's gunboat, January, 1898; present at Battles of Atbara and Omdurman as Intelligence Officer to General Sir Archibald Hunter (severely wounded); served Sudan Campaign of 1899 which suppressed Khalifa Sherif's rising; present at the defeat of the Khalifas at Gedid; assisted in the survey of the Sudan and the Blue Nile; served Boer War as APM and DAAG to Major Lawley's column; Brevet Major, 28th August, 1902; Major, 28th October, 1903; transferred to 6th Dragoon Guards (Carbineers), 1903; Lieutenant Colonel, 6th Dragoon Guards, 1st May, 1909; Colonel, December, 1912; half pay, 1st May, 1913; gained aviator's certificate, 1913; OC Khartoum District, Sudan, 1913-14; Brigadier General commanding 1st Australian Infantry Brigade, Dardanelles, 20th May, 1915-20th December, 1915 (including assault on Lone Pine, 6th August, 1915); served Egypt, 21st December, 1915-18th March, 1916; served Western Front, 1916-18; Major General; OC 58th (London) Division, 1918; OC 59th Division (including Portuguese Artillery and Infantry), 1918-19;

Colonel, 3/6th Dragoon Guards, 1st October, 1920-1925; Hon. Colonel Natal Carbineers; Hon. Colonel 37/39 Battalion Australian Army, 1926; retired, 1924; discharged from the Reserve of Officers, 13th August, 1935.

Rewards, Decorations and Medals: Victoria Cross (for action at Khartoum, 2nd September, 1898); CB; KCB (L.G. 9th June, 1919); Khedive's Sudan Medal (clasps for The Atbara, Firket, Sudan 1897; Khartoum); Queen's Sudan Medal; Queen's South Africa Medal; 1914-15 Star; British War Medal; British Victory Medal (M. in D.); M. in D. for Dongola Expedition, Atbara and Khartoum; Order of the Medjidie (4th Class); Order of Osmanieh (4th Class); Legion of Honour; Commander of the Order of Leopold; Belgian Croix de Guerre.

Post Service Employment: Retired General Officer. The family moved from Cornwall to Melbourne, Australia in 1925.

Married: Evelyn Olwen, daughter of Sir A. Osmond Williams, Bart., MP, of Castell Deudraeth and Borthwen, Merionethshire.

Children: Two sons and one daughter.

Died: Kongbool Homestead, near Balmoral, Victoria, Australia, 21st July, 1941.

Buried: Balmoral Cemetery, Victoria, Australia.

Location of VC: Held by his family.

Citation for VC: L.G. 15th November, 1898.
"At the Battle of Khartoum on the 2nd September, 1898, Captain Smyth galloped forward and attacked an Arab who had run amok among some Camp Followers. Captain Smyth received the Arab's charge, and killed him, being wounded with a spear in the arm in so doing. He thus saved the life of at least one of the Camp Followers."

He was decorated with the VC by H.M. Queen Victoria at Osborne House, Isle of Wight, 6th January, 1899.

N.B. The term 'Camp Follower' in Smyth's VC Citation was inserted by Lord Kitchener. In fact, it referred to the War Correspondents attached to the expedition. The specific Camp Follower whose life he saved was Bennett Burleigh, War Correspondent of the "Daily Telegraph".

Smyth was a cousin of Lord Baden-Powell, founder of the Boy Scout movement.

PRIVATE CHARLES WARD
2nd King's Own Yorkshire Light Infantry

Full Name: Charles Burley Ward.

Place of Birth: 5 Tulip Street, Leeds, Yorkshire.

Date of Birth: 10th July, 1876.

Father: George Ward.

Mother: Ann Ward (nail maker).

Father's Occupation: Labourer.

Education: Primrose Hill School, Leeds.

Pre-Service Employment: –

Service Record: Enlisted King's Own Yorkshire Light Infantry, 29th April, 18 – (Service No. 5480); served Boer War 1899-1900; transferred to 2nd King's Own Yorkshire Light Infantry at Wynberg, Cape Colony; severely wounded at Lindley, 26th June, 1900 (wounds to the head, shoulder, three wounds in one arm, two wounds in other arm, thigh); re-enlisted, Duke of Wellington's (West Riding) Regiment, 10th September, 1914 (Service No. 35893); Drill Instructor at Bristol training 'Kitchener's New Army'; served in France, 1918, as Company Sergeant Major; discharged, 21st November, 1918, as no longer fulfilling the physical requirements of the army; served as Sergeant Major, 3rd Volunteer Battalion, West Yorkshire Regiment.

Rewards, Decorations and Medals: Victoria Cross (for action at Lindley, Orange Free State, South Africa, 26th June, 1900); Queen's South Africa Medal (clasps for Cape Colony and Orange Free State); British War Medal; Victory Medal; received a Testimonial and £600 plus commemorative gold medal from the City of Leeds.

Post-Service Employment: He owned his own newsagents and tobacconist shop in Church Street, Hunslet, Leeds from 1902-1908. He then became a teacher of Physical Education at Bridgend Grammar School, Bridgend, Glamorgan until 1914. He returned to this profession after the war teaching at Barry County School, Barry, Glamorgan.

Married: 1) Emily Kaye, at Hunslet Parish Church, Leeds, 6th October, 1904. He resided at 1 Church Street, Hunslet at this time. They separated towards the end of the Great War. She committed suicide in 1919. 2) Annie Elizabeth McNally, at Cardiff in 1919.

Children: One son and three daughters.

Died: Glamorgan County Asylum, Bridgend, 27th December, 1921. His home address at this time was 3 Soberton Avenue, Cardiff.

Buried: St. Mary's Churchyard, Whitchurch, Cardiff.

Memorials: −

Location of VC: With private collector.

Citation for VC: L.G. 28th September, 1900.

"On 26th June, 1900 at Lindley, a picquet of the Yorkshire Light Infantry was surrounded on three sides by about 500 Boers at close quarters. The two officers were wounded and all but six of the men were killed or wounded. Private Ward then volunteered to take a message asking for reinforcements to the signalling station about 150 yards in the rear of the post. His offer was at first refused, owing to the practical certainty of his being shot; but on his insisting, he was allowed to go. He got across untouched through a storm of shots from each flank and, having delivered his message, he voluntarily returned from a place of absolute safety and recrossed the fire swept ground to assure his Commanding Officer that the message had been sent. On this occasion he was severely wounded. But for this gallant action the post would certainly have been captured."

He was decorated with the VC by H.M. Queen Victoria at Windsor Castle, 15th December, 1900. His was the last VC to be presented by the Queen before she died.

LIEUTENANT LLEWELYN PRICE-DAVIES
1st King's Royal Rifle Corps

Full Name: Llewelyn Almeric Emilius Price-Davies.

Place of Birth: Marrington Hall, Chirbury, Shropshire.

Date of Birth: 30th June, 1878.

Father: Lewis Richard Price.

Mother: Elizabeth Price, daughter of J. J. Turner, J.P., D.L., of Pentrahylin, Montgomeryshire.

Father's Occupation: Landowner.

Education: Marlborough School (Cotton House), April 1892-December, 1894; The Manor House School, Lee, 1895; RMA Sandhurst, January, 1896-January, 1897 (Drill Prize).

Service Record: Commissioned 2nd Lieutenant King's Royal Rifle Corps, 23rd February, 1898; Lieutenant, 21st October, 1899; served Boer War, 1899-1902; relief column for Ladysmith, present at Battle of Colenso, 15th December, 1899; served operations in Natal, 17th-24th January, 1900; present at Spion Kop, 24th January, 1900; served operations in Natal, 5th-7th February, 1900 (present at Val Kranz); served operations in Natal, 14th-27th February, 1900 (present at Tugela Heights and Pieter's Hill); served operations in Natal, March-June, 1900 (present at Laing's Nek, 6th-9th June, 1900); served operations in the Transvaal, east of Pretoria, July-August, 1900; served operations in Transvaal, January-April, 1901; served in operations in Zululand/Natal frontier, September, 1901; served Transvaal and Orange River Colony, April, 1901-May, 1902 (wounded slightly, 17th September, 1901 and severely, 26th January, 1902); Adjutant, 24th Mounted Infantry, South Africa, 25th April, 1901-3rd May, 1901; Captain, 7th January, 1902; Adjutant and QM to the School of Mounted Infantry (Irish Command), 22nd March, 1906-30th September, 1906; Adjutant to 5th Mounted Infantry, South Africa, 1st October, 1906-26th November, 1907; Staff College, Camberley, 1908-09; Brigade Major, 13th Brigade (Irish Command), 1st November, 1910-17th June, 1912; GSO 3, War Office, 18th June, 1912-4th August, 1914; GSO 3, 2nd Division, 4th August, 1914-24th September, 1914; GSO 2, GHQ (France), 2nd October, 1914-10th March, 1915; GSO 2, 4th Division, 11th March, 1915-24th November, 1915; Major, 1st September, 1915; Temporary Brigadier General, 25th November, 1915; GOC 38th Welsh Division, December, 1915-November, 1917; Brevet Lieutenant Colonel, 1st January, 1916; Brigade Commander, France, 3rd April, 1918-11th April, 1918; Special Liaison Officer to Italy, 19th April, 1918-4th November, 1918; Temporary Major-General, 19th April, 1918-15th October, 1919; Brevet Colonel, 3rd June, 1918; President, Standing Committee regarding Prisoners of War; AAG, Aldershot, 9th January, 1920-22nd March, 1924; GOC 145th Infantry Brigade, 23rd March, 1924-24th February, 1927; Brigadier (substantive rank backdated to 3rd June, 1918); GOC Gibraltar (Acting), Local Brigadier, 5th August, 1929-23rd September, 1930; retired, 15th April, 1930, Hon. Major General; HM Body Guard of Hon. Gentlemen at Arms, July, 1933; Battalion Commander, Home Guard, 1939-45.

Rewards, Decorations and Medals: Victoria Cross (for action at Blood River Poort, Transvaal, 17th September, 1901); DSO (for services in South Africa, 1st April, 1901); CMG (L.G. January, 1918); CB (L.G. January, 1921); ADC to H.M. King George V (1920-1930); Queen's South Africa Medal (clasps for Tugela Heights, Orange Free State, Relief of Ladysmith, Transvaal and Laing's Nek); King's South Africa Medal (clasps for 1901 and 1902); M. in D. (South Africa); 1914 Star (with clasp 5th August-22nd November, 1914); British War Medal; Victory Medal (M. in D.); Jubilee Medal (1935); Coronation Medal (1937); Coronation Medal (1953); Legion of Honour (4th Class); Commendatore of the Order of St. Mairizio and St. Lazzaro.

Post Service Employment: Secretary of the Odney Club, Cookham, Hampshire until his retirement in 1945; Vice-President Cookham British Legion; Vice-President YMCA War Committee; committee member of Celer et Audax Club; Life Member Royal British Legion; President, Hounslow Branch, Old Contemptibles Association; Joint Treasurer YMCA; committee member YMCA National Council; involved with the Boy Scouts Association.

Married: Eileen Geraldine Edith, daughter of James Wilson, D.L., of Currygrane, Edgworthstone, Ireland, 8th August, 1906. She was the sister of Field Marshal Sir Henry Wilson.

Children: None.

Died: Corndon, Sonning-on-Thames, Berkshire, 26th December, 1965.

Buried: St. Andrew's Church, Sonning-on-Thames, Berkshire.

Memorials: St. Andrew's Church, Sonning-on-Thames; Winchester Cathedral, Distinguished Service Memorials of the King's Royal Rifle Corps.

Location of VC: King's Royal Rifle Corps Museum, Peninsula Barracks, Winchester, Hampshire.

Citation for VC: L.G. 29th November, 1901.

"At Blood River Poort, South Africa, on the 17th September, 1901, when the Boers had overwhelmed the right of the British column, and some four hundred of them were galloping round the flank and rear of the guns, riding up to the drivers (who were trying to get the guns away) and calling upon them to surrender, Lieutenant Price-Davies, hearing an order to fire upon the charging Boers, at once drew his revolver and dashed upon them in a most gallant and desperate attempt to rescue the guns. He was immediately shot and knocked off his horse, but was not mortally wounded, although he had ridden to what seemed to be certain death without a moment's hesitation."

He was decorated with the VC by General Kitchener at Pretoria, 8th June, 1902.

LANCE CORPORAL WILLIAM FULLER
2nd Welch Regiment

Full Name: William Charles Fuller.

Place of Birth: Newbridge, Laugharne, Carmarthenshire.

Date of Birth: 13th (or 24th) March, 1884.

Father: William Fuller.

Mother: Mary Fuller.

Father's Occupation: Sailor.

Education: Rutland Street School, Swansea; Swansea Truant School, Bonymaen.

Pre-Service Employment: Cinema Caretaker, Swansea.

Service Record: Enlisted, Welch Regiment, 31st December, 1902 (Service No. 7753); served South Africa and India; discharged to the Reserve; recalled 4th August, 1914; served France 12th August, 1914-30th October, 1914 (severely wounded near Gheluvelt, arm and leg wound, 29th October, 1914); invalided home; Lance Corporal, 14th September, 1914; employed as Recruiting Sergeant in Wales; discharged 31st December, 1915, unfit for military service; served as a Warden in Swansea during the Second World War.

Rewards, Decorations and Medals: Victoria Cross (for action near Chivy-sur-Aisne, France, 14th September, 1914); 1914 Star (with clasp 5th August-22nd November, 1914); British War Medal; Victory Medal (M. in D.); Coronation Medal (1937); Coronation Medal (1953); Royal Humane Society Medal for Lifesaving (for saving the lives of two boys aged 7 and 5 at Swansea, 7th June, 1938, they had fallen into the sea); received Exchequer Bonds at Tenby, 1916 bought by a collection from the inhabitants of West Wales.

Post-Service Employment: Proprietor of horse-drawn fish cart, Swansea.

Married: Mary Elizabeth Phillips at Swansea, 1909.

Children: One son and three daughters.

Died: At his home, 55 Westbury Street, Swansea, 29th December, 1974.

Buried: Oystermouth Cemetery, Mumbles, Swansea, 2nd January, 1975. Grave 373 Section R.

Memorials: None recorded.

Location of VC: Held by his family.

Citation for VC: L.G. 23rd November, 1914.

"For conspicuous gallantry on 14th September, near Chivy on the Aisne, by advancing about 100 yards to pick up Captain Haggard, who was mortally wounded, and carrying him back to cover under very heavy rifle and machine-gun fire."

He was decorated with the VC by H.M. King George V at Buckingham Palace, 13th January, 1915.

N.B. The Captain Haggard whose life Fuller tried to save was the nephew of the author Sir Rider Haggard.

ABLE SEAMAN WILLIAM WILLIAMS
HMS River Clyde

Full Name: William Charles Williams.

Place of Birth: Stanton Lacy, Shropshire. The family later lived at 11 Nelson Street, Chepstow, Monmouthshire.

Date of Birth: 15th September, 1880.

Father: William Williams (of Chepstow, Monmouthshire).

Mother: Elizabeth Williams.

Father's Occupation: Gardener.

Education: Chepstow Grammar School.

Pre-Service Employment: Labourer, residing at The Gardens, Chepstow, Monmouthshire.

Service Record: Enlisted for Boy's Service in the Royal Navy at Portsmouth, 17th December, 1895; Service No. ON 186774; Boy 2nd Class, HMS Impregnable, 17th December, 1895-20th December, 1895; HMS Lion, 21st December, 1895-16th September, 1896; Boy 1st Class, HMS Lion, 17th September, 1896; HMS Inflexible, 11th May, 1897; HMS Majestic, 8th June, 1897; HMS Vernon, 1st July, 1898; Ordinary Seaman, HMS Vernon, 15th September, 1898; HMS Victory, 18th September, 1898; HMS Raleigh, 1st November, 1898; HMS Trafalgar, 13th May, 1899; HMS Terrible, 5th September, 1899; landed with the Naval Brigade in South Africa, 1899, recommended for bravery by the Officer in Command; Able Seaman, 14th April, 1900; served in China, 1900, recommended for bravery by the Officer in Command; HMS Glory, 19th July, 1902; HMS Humber, 30th July, 1902; HMS Tamar, 2nd April, 1903; HMS Fire Queen, 16th October, 1903; HMS Vernon, 24th April, 1904; HMS Fire Queen, 18th September, 1904; HMS Furious, 19th February, 1905; HMS Fire Queen, 23rd March, 1905; HMS Victory, 1st April, 1905; HMS Spartiate, 5th December, 1905; HMS Hampshire, 20th August, 1907; HMS Vernon, 1st April, 1909; HMS Victory, 2nd May, 1909; HMS Terrible, 6th June, 1909; HMS Renown, 1st July, 1909; HMS Victory, 1st October, 1909; HMS Furious, 31st October, 1909; HMS Victory, 14th September, 1910; service expired, 14th September, 1910, transferred to the Royal Fleet Reserve (Service No. B3766); HMS Vernon, 19th September, 1910-25th September, 1910; HMS Vernon, 10th March, 1912-16th March, 1912; HMS Vernon, 31st August, 1913-6th September, 1913; recalled to active service, HMS Equant, 28th August, 1914; HMS Hussar, 22nd September, 1914; HMS River Clyde, 25th April, 1915; present at landings at V Beach, Gallipoli, 25th April, 1915.

Rewards, Decorations and Medals: Victoria Cross (for action at V Beach, Gallipoli, 25th April, 1915); Queen's South Africa Medal (clasps for Relief of Ladysmith and Tugela Heights); China Medal, 1900 (clasp, none recorded); 1914-15 Star; British War Medal; Victory Medal; two Good Conduct Badges; he received a grant with his Q.S.A. and China Medals; a Bronze Medallion was presented to his sister by the town of Chepstow.

Post-Service Employment: During the period while he was out of the Royal Navy (1910-14) he was employed at Messrs. Lysaght's Orb Works, Newport, Monmouthshire.

Married: Not married.

Children: None.

Died: K. in A. V Beach, Gallipoli, 25th April, 1915.

Buried: Gallipoli. No known grave.

Memorials: Portsmouth Naval Memorial, MR3, Panel 8; Painting of HMS River Clyde in Chepstow Parish Church; Gun in Beaufort Square, Chepstow, Monmouthshire.

Location of VC: Private collector.

Citation for VC: L.G. 16th August, 1915.
"Held on to a line, in the water, for over an hour under heavy fire until killed."
Due to the brevity of this citation it is necessary to provide further details of A/S Williams' gallantry. Whilst trying to land troops on V Beach, Gallipoli, on 25th April, 1915, HMS River Clyde (a converted collier used as a Troop Landing Ship) came under heavy fire from the enemy. The ship's commander, Commander Unwin, found the current was moving the landing bridge and decided to enter the water in order to secure a rope between himself and the bridge to prevent the latter being washed away. Williams joined him in the water and remained there, repeating the exercise, under a very heavy fire, until, over an hour later, he was hit. Unwin caught him as he fell and Williams died in the Commander's arms. Unwin later called Williams the bravest sailor that he had ever known. Williams was the first lower decker to receive the VC in 50 years. His was also the first ever posthumous award to the Royal Navy.

The VC was presented by H.M. King George V to his parents at Buckingham Palace, 16th November, 1916.

LIEUTENANT COLONEL CHARLES DOUGHTY-WYLIE
Royal Welch Fusiliers

Full Name: Charles Hotham Montagu Doughty (he assumed the additional surname of Wylie by Deed Poll after his marriage in 1904).

Place of Birth: Theberton Hall, Theberton, Leiston, Suffolk. The family also resided at 5 Gloucester Place, Marylebone, London.

Date of Birth: 23rd July, 1868.

Father: Henry Montagu Doughty, J.P.

Mother: Edith Rebecca, daughter of David Cameron, Chief Justice of Vancouver Island, Canada.

Father's Occupation: Barrister (Lincoln's Inn), J.P. for Suffolk, Lord of the Manor of Theberton, Retired Naval Officer.

Education: Winchester; RMA Sandhurst, September, 1888-September, 1889.

Service Record: Commissioned 2nd Lieutenant, Royal Welch Fusiliers, 21st September, 1889; Lieutenant, 23rd September, 1891; served Hazara Expedition (N.W. Frontier), 1891 (severely wounded); served Chitral Relief Force (Himalayas), 1895; present at the occupation of Crete, 1896; Captain, 9th September, 1896; served Nile Expedition, 1898 (present at the Battle of Khartoum); served Nile Expedition, 1899 as Brigade Major with the Flying Column; served South Africa, 1899-1900 as OC regiment of Mounted Infantry (severely wounded at Stinkhoutboom, 24th July, 1900); served Tien Tsin, China where he raised a regiment of Mounted Infantry, 1900; Special Service Officer, Somaliland Operations, 14th January, 1903-June, 1904; Major, 21st August, 1907; Acting Vice-Consul, Mersyna and Konieh, Turkey, 26th September, 1906-3rd December, 1909; Brevet Lieutenant Colonel during his service in Turkey of which a correspondent wrote, "On his own responsibility he assumed practical command of the city of Adana, and by his courage and capacity saved the lives of hundreds — indeed, it was believed by those best able to judge, thousands of many nationalities . . . Wearing his military uniform, he rode through the town with a half-company of Turkish troops, compelling the raging mob to stop killing, and posting guards over particular houses. His right arm was broken by a bullet, but this did not prevent him from riding out again, and in the second and worst outbreak of massacre again saving hundreds of lives"; British Consul, Addis Abbaba, 4th December, 1909-January, 1912 (Charge d'Affaires); Director, British Red Cross, Balkan Campaign, 1912-13; British Representative, International Commission for the De-Limitation of the Southern Frontier of Albania, 29th August, 1913-21st December, 1913 (elected President); GSO 2; Temporary Lieutenant Colonel, 29th August, 1913; British Consul, Addis Abbaba, December, 1913-April, 1914; Charge d'Affaires, Addis Abbaba, 1st April, 1914-24th January, 1915; Lieutenant Colonel, 31st January, 1915; GSO 2 (War Office), 22nd February, 1915; posted to the Staff of Sir Ian Hamilton, Mediterranean Expeditionary Force; served Gallipoli, April, 1915.

Rewards, Decorations and Medals: Victoria Cross (for action at Old Fort, Hill 41, Sedd-el-Bahr, Gallipoli, 26th April, 1915); CB (L.G. 22nd June, 1914, for services as a member of the Albanian Delimitation Commission — Civil Award); CMG (L.G. 25th June, 1909, for services during the disturbances in Asia Minor); Indian General Service Medal, 1854-95 (clasp for Hazama, 1891); India Medal, 1895-1902 (clasp for Relief of Chitral, 1895); Queen's Sudan Medal, 1896-97; Queen's South Africa Medal (clasps for Wittebergen, Transvaal and Cape Colony); Africa General Service Medal, 1902-56 (clasp for Somaliland, 1902-04); 1914-15 Star; British War Medal; Victory Medal; Order of the Medjidie (2nd Class, Turkey); Order of the Medjidie (5th Class, Turkey); Order of the Star (3rd Class, Ethiopia).

Married: Lilian Oimera, daughter of John Wylie of Glasgow and West Clyffe Hall, Hampshire, widow of Lieutenant Charles Henry Adams, Indian Medical Service, 1st June, 1904. (She was the only British woman to visit the battlefield at Gallipoli during the fighting. She was later awarded the OBE and the Royal Red Cross for her work with the British Red Cross Society.)

Children: None recorded.

Died: 26th April, 1915, at the Old Fort, Hill 41, Sedd-el-Bahr, Gallipoli.

Buried: Where he fell, at midnight, 26th April, 1915. It is an isolated military grave.

Memorials: V Beach Cemetery, Gallipoli; St. Peter's Church and Churchyard, Theberton, Suffolk (memorial window); War Memorial, Theberton, Suffolk; Cybi Hall, Holyhead, Anglesey.

Location of VC: RWF Museum, Caernarfon Castle, Caernarfon.

Citation for VC: L.G. 23rd June, 1915.

"On 26th April, 1915, subsequent to a landing having been affected on the beach at a point on the Gallipoli peninsula, during which both Brigadier-General and Brigade Major had been killed, Lieutenant Colonel Doughty-Wylie and Captain Walford organised and led an attack through and on both sides of the village of Sedd-el-Bahr on the Old Castle at the top of the hill inland. The enemy's position was very strongly entrenched and defended with concealed machine guns and pom-poms.

"It was mainly due to the initiative, skill and great gallantry of these two officers that the attack was a complete success. Both were killed in the moment of victory."

The VC was presented to his widow by H.M. King George V at Buckingham Palace, 8th March, 1921.

N.B. Captain Garth Neville Walford, RRA, who led the assault with Lt. Colonel Doughty-Wylie, was also awarded a posthumous Victoria Cross for his gallantry in this attack.

CSM FREDERICK BARTER
1st Royal Welch Fusiliers (Special Reserve)

Full Name: Frederick Barter.

Place of Birth: 60 Daniel Street, Cathays, Cardiff.

Date of Birth: 17th January, 1891.

Father: Samuel Barter.

Mother: —

Father's Occupation: —

Education: Crwys Road Board School, Cardiff.

Pre-Service Employment: Wagon Works, Cardiff; Collier; Porter, Great Western Railway; Stove repairer, Cardiff Gas Light and Coke Company.

Service Record: Enlisted Royal Welch Fusiliers, 4th December, 1908 (Service No. 3902); transferred to Royal Welch Fusiliers Special Reserve; mobilised

1st Royal Welch Fusiliers, 5th August, 1914; Company Sergeant Major (1914); served France, 1914-15; commissioned 2nd Lieutenant, Royal Welch Fusiliers, 26th August, 1915; employed Western Command Bombing School, 10th May, 1916-29th December, 1916 (Temporary Lieutenant); served France, December, 1916-February, 1917; seconded for service with the Indian Army, 16th March, 1917; served Queen Alexandra's Own Gurkha Rifles, at Kohat, North-West Frontier Province; Brigade Bombing Officer; served Palestine with 2/3rd Queen Alexandra's Own Gurkha Rifles, December, 1917-January, 1919 (Acting Captain); relinquished commission in Royal Welch Fusiliers on permanent commission in the Indian Army, 6th May, 1918; invalided to U.K., January, 1919 with fever; retired as Captain, 1922; Major commanding t4/7 Company, 4th Middlesex Home Guard during Second World War.

Rewards, Decorations and Medals: Victoria Cross (for action at Festubert, France, 16th May, 1915); Military Cross (for action at El Kefr, Palestine, 10th April, 1918); 1914 Star, British War Medal; Victory Medal (M. in D.); Coronation Medal (1937).

Post-Service Employment: After retiring from the army he tried one or two private ventures. In 1928 he joined the AEC where he was employed as a Labour Manager at Southall until his death.

Married: Catherine Mary Theresa Maclaren (nee Wright), divorcee, 13th May, 1925. She was the proprietress of the Heathfield Hotel, Waldron. She died in 1944.

Children: None recorded.

Died: St. Ann's Nursing Home, Canford Cliffe, Poole, Dorset, 15th May, 1953.

Buried: Cremated at Bournemouth Crematorium, ashes scattered in the Garden of Remembrance.

Memorials: Barter Road and Barter Court, Hightown, Wrexham, Clwyd.

Location of VC: Private collector, North America.

Citation for VC: L.G. 29th June, 1915.
"For most conspicuous bravery and marked ability at Festubert on 16th May, 1915. When in the first line of German trenches, Company Sergeant Major Barter called for volunteers to enable him to extend our line and with eight men who responded he attacked the German position with bombs, capturing three German officers and 102 men and 500 yards of their trenches. He subsequently found and cut eleven of the enemy's mine leads, situated about twenty yards apart."

He was decorated with the VC by H.M. King George V at Buckingham Palace, 12th July, 1915.

Citation for MC: L.G. 26th July, 1918.
"For conspicuous gallantry and devotion to duty when ordered to make a flank attack. He led his two platoons up a precipitous hill, and turned the enemy's flank. Then, placing one platoon with two Lewis guns to command the enemy's line of retreat, he gallantly led an attack with the other platoon from the rear and flank, killing or capturing practically the whole garrison."

N.B. At El Kefr, 10th April, 1918, Barter's life was saved by Rifleman Karanbahadur Rana who was subsequently awarded the Victoria Cross for his gallantry.

TEMPORARY 2nd LIEUTENANT RUPERT HALLOWES
4th Middlesex Regiment

Full Name: Rupert Price Hallowes.

Place of Birth: Checkley, Redhill, Surrey.

Date of Birth: 5th May, 1881.

Father: Dr. Frederick Blackwood Hallowes, F.R.C.S.

Mother: Mary Ann Taylor Hallowes (daughter of Rev. W. Hutchinson, Rector of Checkley, Staffordshire).

Father's Occupation: General Practitioner, Messrs. Martin, Holman and Hallowe⁻, Redhill.

Education: Conyngham House, Ramsgate; Haileybury College, Hertfordshire (shot fo· the school at Bisley in 1896 and 1897, member of the O.T.C.).

Pre-Service Employment: Hull, Blythe and Co., London (until 1909); Assistant Works Manager, Robert Byass & Co. Ltd., Mansel Works, Aberavon, Glamorgan (at this time he lived at Pen-Y-Cae, Port Talbot). In his spare time he was an instructor in St. Peter's Troop of the Boy Scout Association in Port Talbot and Hon. Secretary of the Church of England Men's Society in Port Talbot.

Service Record: Enlisted as a Private in the Artist's Rifles, Territorial Army, c.1900; commissioned 2nd Lieutenant, Artist's Rifles, 17th November, 1909; resigned his commission on moving to South Wales, c.1910; re-enlisted in the Artist's Rifles (then attached to the 4th Middlesex Regiment) as a Private, 5th August, 1914; promoted to Sergeant by 13th August, 1914; posted overseas, 27th December, 1914; commissioned Temporary 2nd Lieutenant, Middlesex Regiment, 7th April, 1915; home leave, July, 1915; attended Bombing School, September, 1915.

Rewards, Decorations and Medals: Victoria Cross (for action at Hooge, Belgium, between 25th and 30th September, 1915); Military Cross (for action at Hooge, Belgium, 19th/20th July, 1915); 1914-15 Star; British War Medal; Victory Medal (M. in D.).

Married: Not married.

Children: None.

Died: K. in A. at Hooge, Belgium, 30th September, 1915.

Buried: Initially in an isolated grave at Sanctuary Wood, 1st October, 1915. Re-interred at Bedford House Cemetery, Zillebeke, near Ypres, Belgium, Enclosure 4, Plot 16, Row B, Grave 36.

Memorials: Bedford House Cemetery, Zillebeke, Belgium; gateway to Port Talbot Public Park, Port Talbot, Glamorgan; Haileybury College Chapel; Royal Ancient Order of Buffalos Lodge, Port Talbot, Glamorgan was named 'Rupert Hallowes VC Lodge'; ward and X-ray Department at Aberavon General Hospital named after him (paid for by the works staff of Robert Byass & Co. Ltd., and Port Talbot Boy Scouts Association); portrait in St. Theadore's Mission Room, Port Talbot, Glamorgan.

Location of VC: Middlesex Regiment.

Citation for VC: L.G. 18th November, 1915.

"For most conspicuous bravery and devotion to duty during the fighting at Hooge between 25th September and 1st October, 1915.

"Second Lieutenant Hallowes displayed throughout these days the greatest bravery and untiring energy, and set a magnificent example to his men during four heavy and prolonged bombardments. On more than one occasion he climbed up the parapet, utterly regardless of danger, in order to put fresh heart into his men. He made daring reconnaissances of the German positions in our lines. When the supply of bombs was running short he went back under very heavy shell fire and brought up a fresh supply. Even after he was mortally wounded he continued to cheer those around him and to inspire them with fresh courage."

The VC was presented to his mother by H.M. King George V at Buckingham Palace, 29th November, 1916.

Citation for MC: L.G. 6th September, 1915.

"For conspicuous gallantry on the night of 19th July, 1915, at Hooge, when, owing to the shortage of bombs, the enemy were advancing down the Communication Trench. He got out of his trench, exposing himself fearlessly, and fired at the enemy in the open, hitting several. He also assisted in making a block, dug out a Communication Trench under heavy shell fire, and rebuilt a parapet that had been blown in. Throughout the night he assisted in keeping touch and supplying bombs."

CORPORAL SAMUEL MEEKOSHA
1/6th West Yorkshire Regiment

Full Name: Samuel Meekosha (in 1941, he changed his surname, by Deed Poll, to Ingham).

Place of Birth: 3 High Street, Leeds, Yorkshire. The family later moved to 91 Tennant Street, West Bowling, Bradford.

Date of Birth: 16th September, 1893.

Father: Alexander Meekosha (a Polish immigrant).

Mother: Mary Meekosha (nee Cunningham).

Father's Occupation: Tailor.

Education: St. Joseph's R.C. School, Bradford.

Pre-Service Employment: Office worker for a manufacturing company in Bradford.

Service Record: Enlisted in the 1/6th West Yorkshire Territorial Regiment, 20th February, 1911 (Service No. 1147); mobilised 5th August, 1914; served France and Belgium, 15th April, 1915-November, 1916; Corporal, 13th February, 1915; Sergeant, 15th November, 1915; re-signed, 15th December, 1915; commissioned 2nd Lieutenant, 26th June, 1917; served France and Belgium, 15th August, 1917-19th December, 1917; Lieutenant, 27th December, 1918; Captain, 15th May, 1919; transferred to Corps of Military Accountants, 19th November, 1919; Captain and Account Officer 6th Class, 31st January, 1920; retired, 17th March, 1926; commissioned Royal Army Ordnance Corps, 15th January, 1940; transferred to Regular Army Reserve of Officers, 6th October, 1944 rank of Major; discharged from the Reserve of Officers, 6th October, 1948.

Rewards, Decorations and Medals: Victoria Cross (for action near Yser, France, 19th November, 1915); 1914-15 Star; British War Medal; Victory Medal; Coronation Medal (1937); Defence Medal; British War Medal (1939-45).

Post-Service Employment: Owned a wholesale tobacco business in Bradford for a period between the wars; Sales Representative, John Player and Sons, covering South Wales, from 1930 (he resided for a time in Penarth,

Glamorgan and later at Penrhiw Villas, Oakdale, Monmouthshire).

Married: 1) Bertha Elizabeth Duval of Bradford; 2) Constance Ingham of Leeds.

Children: Two sons and one daughter by his first wife.

Died: 8th December, 1950 at Blackwood, Monmouthshire.

Buried: Cremated at Pontypridd Crematorium.

Memorials: None known.

Location of VC: Held by the family.

Citation for VC: L.G. 22nd January, 1916.

"For most conspicuous bravery near Yser on the 19th November, 1915. He was with a platoon of about twenty Non-commissioned Officers and men, who were holding an isolated trench. During a very heavy bombardment by the enemy, six of the platoon were killed and seven wounded, while all the remainder were more or less buried.

"When the senior Non-commissioned Officers had been either killed or wounded, Corporal Meekosha at once took command, sent a runner for assistance, and in spite of no less than ten more big shells falling within twenty yards of him, continued to dig out the wounded and buried men in full view of the enemy, and at close range from the German trenches. By his promptness and magnificent courage and determination he saved at least four lives."

He was decorated with the VC by H.M. King George V at Buckingham Palace, 4th March, 1916.

2nd LIEUTENANT EDGAR MYLES
8th Welch Regiment, attached Worcestershire Regiment

Full Name: Edgar Kinghorn Myles.

Place of Birth: Blackhall Crescent, Wanstead, Essex.

Date of Birth: 29th July, 1894.

Father: Andrew Kinghorn Myles.

Mother: Agnes Jane Myles.

Father's Occupation: —

Education: East Ham Council School, Shrewsbury Road; East Ham Technical College.

Pre-Service Employment: Clerk, Port of London Authority.

Service Record: Enlisted, 9th Worcestershire Regiment, 20th August, 1914 (Service No. 9311); discharged with the rank of Lance Corporal on application for commission, 27th November, 1914; Temporary 2nd Lieutenant, Worcestershire Regiment, 28th November, 1914; 2nd Lieutenant, Welch Regiment, with seniority from 4th December, 1915; served Gallipoli, August, 1915-January, 1916 (with the rearguard at the evacuation from Sulva Bay, Gallipoli); served Mesopotamia, March, 1916-April, 1918 (wounded twice), present at the attempt to relieve Kut; Acting Captain, 21st October, 1916; transferred to Worcestershire Regiment, seniority from 28th August, 1915, as 2nd Lieutenant, 12th January, 1917; Lieutenant, with seniority from 19th October, 1916, 12th January, 1917; Temporary Captain, 19th January, 1917; GSO 3 Intelligence Department, War Office, October, 1919-April, 1920; seconded to Royal Tank Corps, 5th December,

1921;transferred to King's Liverpool Regiment as Lieutenant with seniority from 19th October, 1916, 9th May, 1923; Captain, 22nd February, 1925; retired 10th March, 1928; re-employed, 9th April, 1939; unemployed, 22nd January, 1940; ARP Officer, Leyton, London, January, 1938; ARP Officer, Islington, London, April, 1938.

Rewards, Decorations and Medals: Victoria Cross (for action at Sanna-I-Yat, Mesopotamia, 9th April, 1916); DSO (for action 25th January, 1917); 1914-15 Star; British War Medal; Victory Medal (M. in D.); Coronation Medal (1937); Coronation Medal (1953).

Post-Service Employment: —

Married: Ellen M. Illingworth (or Carr) at Hatfield, 1947.

Children: None recorded.

Died: 1st February, 1977 at Bishopsteignton, Devon. During the latter part of his life, Myles was living in an almost destitute state in a converted railway carriage with his dog. His situation was discovered and he was placed in the Huntley British Legion Home in Bishopsteignton, Devon, where he died shortly afterwards.

Buried: Cremated at Torquay Crematorium.

Memorials: None recorded.

Location of VC: Worcestershire Regimental Museum, Worcester.

Citation for VC: L.G. 26th September, 1916.

"For most conspicuous bravery. He went out alone on several occasions in front of our advanced trenches and, under heavy rifle fire, at great personal risk, assisted wounded men lying in the open. On one occasion he carried in a wounded officer to a place of safety under circumstances of great danger."

He was decorated with the VC by H.M. King George V at Buckingham Palace, 4th September, 1918.

Citation for DSO: L.G. 17th March, 1917.

"When all the officers except two had become casualties, he, for five hours, inspired confidence in the defence against 2 counter-attacks, also sending back most accurate and valuable reports of the situation. His courage and fine example were largely responsible for the steadiness of all ranks with him."

N.B. General Maud, GOC troops at the Relief of Kut, informed Myles, when presenting him with the DSO, that it had been his intention to recommend him for a second VC but did not wish to create a precedent and therefore recommended him for the DSO instead.

TEMPORARY CAPTAIN ANGUS BUCHANAN
4th South Wales Borderers

Full Name: Angus Buchanan.

Place of Birth: Old Bank House, Coleford, Gloucestershire.

Date of Birth: 11th August, 1894.

Father: Dr. Peter Buchanan, M.D., C.M., J.P., V.D.

Mother: Hannah Allen Buchanan (nee Williams).

Father's Occupation: Medical Practitioner at Coleford; Deputy Coroner, Forest of Dean; Major, 2nd Volunteer Battalion, Gloucestershire Regiment.

Education: St. John's Boys' School, Coleford; Monmouth Grammar School (where he was a good, all-round sportsman, won the essay prize three years running, Colour Sergeant in the Cadet Corps, Captain of the School, Rugby Captain, School Cricket Team, School Rowing Crew). Scholarship to Jesus College, Oxford (played in University Rugby trials and Oxford University 'A' Team 1913-14, Officer Training Corps).

Service Career: Commissioned Temporary 2nd Lieutenant, South Wales Borderers, 27th November, 1914; Temporary Lieutenant, 28th June, 1915; Temporary Captain, 21st December, 1915; Regular Commission, 2nd September, 1917; retired 2nd September, 1917 due to wounds received (which resulted in his being blinded for life); appointed Hon. Captain, 2nd September, 1917; served Gallipoli; served Mesopotamia (wounded 5th April, 1916 and 13th February, 1917, hospitalised in India).

Rewards, Decorations and Medals: Victoria Cross (for action at Falauyah Lines, Mesopotamia, 5th April, 1916); Military Cross (for action at Cape Helles, Gallipoli, 7th January, 1916, L.G. 3rd June, 1916); Order of St. Vladimir (4th Class) with swords (L.G. 15th May, 1917); 1914-15 Star; British War Medal; Victory Medal (M. in D., 1916, four times); Coronation Medal (1937); Gold watch from the people of Coleford.

Post-Service Employment: Studied Law at St. Dunstan's, degree Jesus College (rowed in the College Fours); Solicitor at Coleford, Gloucestershire; Chairman, Coleford Royal British Legion; keen salmon fisherman.

Married: Details not known.

Children: Details not known.

Died: 1st March, 1944, at Coleford, Gloucestershire.

Buried: Coleford, Gloucestershire.

Memorials: Angus Buchanan VC Memorial Gardens, Coleford, Gloucestershire (subscribed for by the people of Coleford).

Location of VC: SWB Museum.

Citation for VC: L.G. 26th September, 1916.
"For most conspicuous bravery. During an attack an Officer was lying out in the open severely wounded about 150 yards from cover. Two men went to his assistance and one of them was hit at once. Captain Buchanan, on seeing this, immediately went out and with the help of the other man, carried the wounded man to cover under heavy machine gun fire. He then returned and brought in the wounded man, again under heavy fire."

He was decorated with the VC by H.M. King George V at Durnham Down, Bristol, 8th November, 1917.

PRIVATE JAMES FINN
1/4th South Wales Borderers

Full Name: James Henry Finn (his army records incorrectly show his surname as being spelt Fynn).

Place of Birth: St. Clements, Truro, Cornwall. The family later resided in Downing Street, Bodmin, Cornwall.

Date of Birth: 24th November, 1893.

Father: Frederick John Finn.

Mother: Mary Baxter Finn (nee Uglow) of Camborne.

Father's Occupation: Cutler (grinder of scissors and tools). He served with the Duke of Cornwall's Light Infantry during the Boer War and again in the Special Reserve during the Great War.

Education: Board School, Bodmin, Cornwall.

Pre-Service Employment: Collier, Cwmtillery, Monmouthshire. He resided in Frederick Street, Cwmtillery.

Service Record: Enlisted in the South Wales Borderers at Abertillery, 1914 (Service No. 1/11220); served at Gallipoli, 1915; served Mesopotamia with 4th South Wales Borderers, 1916-17; servant to Lt. Colonel Kitchin, OC 4th South Wales Borderers; wounded in the knee and chest and invalided back to Britain; rejoined his battalion in Mesopotamia.

Rewards, Decorations and Medals: Victoria Cross (for action at Sanna-i-Yat, Mesopotamia, 9th April, 1916); 1914-15 Star; British War Medal; Victory Medal (M. in D.); Serbian Karageorge, 1st Class (L.G. 15th February, 1917).

Married: Not married.

Children: None.

Died: Died of wounds, Mesopotamia, 30th March, 1917. He was wounded in the leg on 29th March, 1917 at Noel Plain, 50 miles north of Baghdad, and was hit again en route to the Field Ambulance on the following day.

Buried: No known grave.

Memorials: Basra Memorial, Iraq, Panels 16 and 32; Finn VC Estate, Bodmin, Cornwall; The Guildhall, Bodmin, Cornwall.

Location of VC: Bodmin Town Hall, Cornwall.

Citation for VC: L.G. 26th September, 1916.

"For most conspicuous bravery. After a night attack he was one of a small party which dug in, in front of our advanced line and about 300 yards from the enemy's trenches. Seeing several wounded men lying out in front he went out and bandaged them all under heavy fire, making several journeys in order to do so. He then went back to our advanced trench for a stretcher and, being unable to get one, he himself carried on his back a badly wounded man into safety. He then returned and, aided by another man who was wounded during the act, carried in another badly wounded man. He was under continuous fire whilst performing this gallant work."

He was decorated with the ribbon of the VC by Lt. General Sir Stanley Maude, GOC Mesopotamia, at Amarah, November, 1916. The VC was presented to his father at a public investiture in Hyde Park, 2nd June, 1917, by H.M. King George V.

TEMPORARY MAJOR LIONEL REES
Royal Garrison Artillery/No. 32 Squadron Royal Flying Corps

Full Name: Lionel Wilmot Brabazon Rees.

Place of Birth: Plas Llanwnda, Caernarfon, Caernarfonshire.

Date of Birth: 31st July, 1884.

Father: Colonel Charles Herbert Rees, VD.

Mother: Leonora Maria Rees (daughter of Smith William Davids of Caernarfon).

Father's Occupation: Solicitor and officer in the 3rd Volunteer Battalion, Royal Welch Fusiliers.

Education: Ems Colwall Malvern Preparatory School, 1891-95; Eastbourne

College (Blackwater House), March, 1898-March, 1901 (School Prefect, 1st XV, Sergeant in O.T.C., school colours for running and shooting); Royal Military Academy, Woolwich, 1901-03 (winner of Tombs Memorial Prize).

Service Record: Commissioned Royal Garrison Artillery, 23rd December, 1903; Lieutenant, 23rd December, 1906; Aviator's Certificate (No. 392), Royal Aero Club, 7th January, 1913; served on active duties, West African Frontier Force, 21st May, 1913-9th August, 1914; seconded to Royal Flying Corps as Lieutenant, 10th August, 1914; posted to Briges, France, to form an aircraft park, August, 1914; Captain, 30th October, 1914; appointed an Instructor at the Central Flying School, Upavon; Flight Commander, No. 11 Squadron, Netheravon, 14th February, 1915; posted to Vert Galand, Amiens, France, 27th July, 1915; Instructor, Central Flying School, Upavon, November, 1915-February, 1916; Major (with seniority from 28th November, 1915), 1st December, 1916; OC No. 32 Squadron on formation at Netheravon, 1st February, 1916; OC No. 32 Squadron, St. Omer, France, 28th May, 1916 (later based at Auchel, Treizennes and Aire); invalided home, July, 1916 with leg wound received 1st July, 1916, treated at Wilton House Hospital, Salisbury, until 1917; Lieutenant Colonel, 1st May, 1917; War Office Delegate on Balfour Mission to the USA, 1917; OC No. 1 School of Aerial Fighting, Ayr, Scotland (later Turnberry) until the end of hostilities; Lt. Colonel, Royal Air Force, with effect from 26th July, 1919; Wing Commander, 27th August, 1919; Assistant Commandant RAF College, Cranwell, 1923-24; Group Captain, 1st January, 1925; Deputy Director of Training, Air Ministry, 1925; OC Headquarters, RAF Transjordan and Palestine, April, 1926-1929; OC RAF Uxbridge, 1929-30; OC No. 21 Group, 1930-31; retired 1931; re-employed as Wing Commander, 21st January, 1941 (having relinquished the rank of Group Captain at his own request), Service No. 01100; served North Africa, 1941-42; retired 21st November, 1942 (resuming the rank of Group Captain).

Rewards, Decorations and Medals: Victoria Cross (for action in the air during the first day of the Battle of the Somme, 1st July, 1916); Military Cross (for action July-September, 1915); Air Force Cross (for duties as a Flying Instructor, L.G. 2nd November, 1918); OBE (L.G. 3rd June, 1919); ADC to H.M. King George V (1925-31); 1914 Star; British War Medal; Victory Medal (M. in D.); 1939-45 Star; British War Medal (1939-45); Africa Star; Coronation Medal (1937); Coronation Medal (1953); Freeman of the Borough of Caernarfon (15th January, 1920); Sword of Honour (Borough of Caernarfon, 1920); American Deep Sea Medal (1934, for the most outstanding feat of seamanship of the year); RAF Revolver Champion (1923); RAF Foil Champion (1923).

Post-Service Employment: In August 1933, he sailed from Porth-yr-Aur, Caernarfon, in his eight ton boat 'The May' and arrived, sixty-four days later, at Nassau in the Bahamas having crossed the Atlantic single-handed. Apart from his service during the Second World War, he spent the remainder of his life living aboard a boat named 'Aline' at Madeira Cay, Andros, in the Bahamas, where he grew sponges.

Married: Sylvia, daughter of Alexander Williams, at Mangrove Cay, Andros, Bahamas, 12th August, 1947.

Children: Three children. Details unknown.

Died: 28th September, 1955, at Andros, Bahamas.

Buried: Commonwealth War Graves Cemetery, Nassau, Bahamas.

Memorials: Commonwealth War Graves Cemetery, Nassau, Bahamas; Eastbourne College; Council Chamber, Caernarfon, Caernarfonshire; RAF College, Cranwell.

Location of VC: Eastbourne College, Eastbourne.

Citation for VC: L.G. 5th August, 1916.

"For conspicuous gallantry and devotion to duty. Whilst on flying duties, Major Rees sighted what he thought to be a bombing party of our machines returning home. He went up to escort them but, on getting nearer, discovered they were a party of enemy machines, about ten in all. Major Rees was immediately attacked by one of the machines, and after a short encounter it disappeared behind enemy lines, damaged. The others then attacked him at long range, but these he dispersed by coming to close quarters, after seriously damaging two of the machines. Seeing two others going westwards, he gave chase to them, but on coming nearer he was wounded in the thigh, causing him to lose temporary control of his machine. He soon righted it, and immediately closed with the enemy, firing at close range of only a few yards, until all his ammunition was used up. He then returned home landing his machine safely in our lines."

He was decorated with the VC by H.M. King George V at Buckingham Palace, 14th December, 1916.

Citation for Military Cross: L.G. 29th October, 1915.

"For conspicuous gallantry and skill on several occasions, notably the following:—

"On 21st September, 1915, when flying a machine with one machine gun, accompanied by Flight-Serjeant Hargreaves, he sighted a large German biplane with two machine guns 2,000 feet below him. He spiralled down and dived at the enemy, who, having the faster machine, manoeuvered to get him broadside on and then opened fire. In spite of this Captain Rees pressed his attack and apparently succeeded in hitting the enemy's engine, for the machine made a quick turn, glided some distance and finally fell just inside the German lines near Herbecourt.

"On 28th July, he attacked and drove down a hostile monoplane in spite of the fact that the main spar of his machine had been shot through and the rear spar shattered.

"On 31st August, accompanied by Flight-Serjeant Hargreaves, he fought a German machine more powerful than his own for three-quarters of an hour, then returned for more ammunition and went out to attack again, finally bringing the enemy's machine down apparently wrecked."

CORPORAL JOSEPH DAVIES
10th Royal Welch Fusiliers

Full Name: Joseph John Davies.

Place of Birth: Tipton, Staffordshire. The family later resided at 48 Cross Street, Wednesbury, Staffordshire.

Date of Birth: 28th April, 1889.

Father: John Davies.

Mother: Annie Davies.

Father's Occupation: Serviceman, 7th Royal Fusiliers (wounded at Kandahar).

Education: Greatbridge School, Tipton, Staffordshire.

Pre-Service Employment: Colliery worker.

Service Record: Enlisted Welch Regiment, 19th August, 1909 (Service No. 10236); posted to 1st Welch Regiment; served Egypt, 18th January, 1910-27th January, 1914 (one year with the Camel Corps); served India, 28th January, 1914-17th November, 1914; served France and Flanders, 16th January, 1915-10th March, 1915 (wounded); served France and Flanders, 8th May, 1915-23rd August, 1915; wounded July, 1915 (knuckles of both hands smashed by German bayonets); posted to 1st Garrison Battalion, Royal Welch Fusiliers, 11th August, 1915; Lance Corporal, 5th September, 1915; served Gibraltar, 23rd August, 1915-7th May, 1916; Acting Corporal, 10th January, 1916; transferred 3rd Royal Welch Fusiliers, 8th May, 1916 (Service Number 34312); Corporal, April, 1916; transferred to 10th Royal Welch Fusiliers, 1st October, 1916; Sergeant, 6th October, 1916; transferred to 3rd Royal Welch Fusiliers, 27th May, 1917; transferred to Military Provost Staff (unfit for active duty due to severe shoulder wound received during 2nd Battle of Ypres) (Service No. T.1950); Acting Staff Sergeant, 15th March, 1918; reverted to Sergeant, 7th May, 1918; transferred to Army Reserve, 4th June, 1918; discharged, 14th December, 1918; re-enlisted Herefordshire Regiment (Territorial Force), 13th November, 1920 (Service No. 4103165); Sergeant, 13th January, 1921; discharged, 12th November, 1922; served as Regimental Sergeant Major to Poole Cadet Force during the Second World War during which time he was also Chief Warden at Oakdale, Poole, Dorset.

Rewards, Decorations and Medals: Victoria Cross (for action at Delville Wood, France, 20th July, 1916); 1914-15 Star; British War Medal; Victory Medal; Defence Medal; Coronation Medal (1937); Coronation Medal (1953); Russian Order of St. George (1st Class) (L.G. 15th February, 1916).

Married: Elsie Thomas of Presteigne, Herefordshire, 1917.

Children: Two daughters.

Post-Service Employment: Due to the severe injuries which he had received in the Great War he was unable to return to his pre-service employment. He was employed as a Commissionaire by Birmingham Corporation Gas Works and then moved to Poole in Dorset where he was employed by the Holton Heath Cordite Factory. His address was 11 North Road, Parkstone, Poole, then Milne Road, Waterloo, Poole, and finally 2 Trinidad House, Parkstone, Poole.

Died: 23rd February, 1976, at Bournemouth Hospital, Bournemouth, Hampshire.

Buried: Cremated at Bournemouth Crematorium.

Memorials: Greatbridge School, Tipton, Staffordshire; Davies Court, Hightown, Wrexham.

Location of VC: Royal Welch Fusiliers Museum, Caernarfon Castle, Caernarfon.

Citation for VC: L.G. 26th September, 1916.

"For most conspicuous bravery. Prior to an attack on the enemy in a wood he became separated with eight men from the rest of his company. When the enemy delivered their second counter-attack his party was completely surrounded, but he got them into a shell hole, and by throwing bombs and opening rapid fire, succeeded in routing them. Not content with this he followed them up in their retreat and bayonetted several of them. Corporal Davies set a magnificent example of pluck and determination.

He has done other very gallant work and was badly wounded in the Second Battle of Ypres."

He was decorated with the VC by H.M. King George V at Buckingham Palace on 29th October, 1916.

He was decorated with the Russian Order of St. George (1st Class) by General Campbell at Manchester in 1917.

N.B. His family state that, to the end of his life, Joseph Davies claimed to have shot down a German aircraft with a machine gun whilst in the trenches. He also stated that he had been appointed to the position of King's Sergeant as a reward for his gallantry during that war.

PRIVATE ALBERT HILL
10th Royal Welch Fusiliers

Full Name: Albert Hill.

Place of Birth: Hulme, Manchester. The family moved to Peacock Street, Denton, when he was aged 12. He later lived at 45 High Street, Denton.

Date of Birth: 24th May, 1895.

Father: Harry Hill.

Mother: Elizabeth Hill.

Father's Occupation: Collier at Ashton Moss Colliery.

Education: Trinity Wesleyan School, Denton, Nr. Manchester.

Pre-Service Employment: Employed at the Alpha Mill. He was then apprenticed to Joseph Wilson & Sons, Hat Manufacturers of Denton, as a Planker.

Service Record: Enlisted Royal Welch Fusiliers, 3rd August, 1914 (Service No. 15280); served France and Flanders; demobilised circa. February, 1919. Very little is known of his service in the Great War as the records were destroyed by German bombing during the Second World War.

Rewards, Decorations and Medals: Victoria Cross (for action at Delville Wood, France, 20th July, 1916); 1914-15 Star; British War Medal; Victory Medal; Coronation Medal (1937); Coronation Medal (1953); Croix de Guerre (France).

Post-Service Employment: Returned to Joseph Wilson & Sons, Hat Manufacturers of Denton. In 1923 he emigrated to the United States of America residing first in Central Falls. Ten years later he moved to Pawtucket, Rhode Island, where he was employed as a building labourer with H. M. Soule Construction Company until he retired. He resided at 41 Thornley Street, Pawtucket, 117 Maryland Avenue, Pawtucket, and finally at 175 Broad Street, Pawtucket.

Married: Doris May Wilson of Hyde, Cheshire, 14th February, 1920.

Children: One son and three daughters.

Died: 17th February, 1971 at the Memorial Hospital, Pawtucket, Rhode Island.

Buried: Highland Memorial Park, Johnston, Rhode Island, 20th February, 1971.

Memorials: Highland Memorial Park, Johnston, Rhode Island; Hill Court, Hightown, Wrexham.

Location of VC: Royal Welch Fusiliers Museum, Caernarfon Castle, Caernarfon.

Citation for VC: L.G. 26th September, 1916.

"For most conspicuous bravery. When his battalion had deployed under very heavy fire for an attack on the enemy in a wood, he dashed forward, when the order to charge was given and, meeting two of the enemy suddenly, bayonetted them both. He was sent later by his platoon sergeant to get in touch with the company and, finding himself cut off and almost surrounded by some twenty of the enemy, he attacked them with bombs, killing and wounding many and scattering the remainder. He then joined a sergeant of his company and helped him to fight the way back to the lines. When he got back, hearing that his Company Officer and a scout were lying out wounded, he went out and assisted to bring in the wounded officer, two other men bringing in the scout.

"Finally, he himself captured and brought in as prisoners two of the enemy. His conduct throughout was magnificent."

He was decorated with the VC by H.M. King George V at Buckingham Palace, 18th November, 1916.

PRIVATE HUBERT LEWIS
11th (Cardiff Pals) Welch Regiment

Full Name: Hubert William Lewis (on his VC citation his Christian name is incorrectly given as Herbert).

Place of Birth: Robert Street, Milford Haven, Pembrokeshire.

Date of Birth: 1st May, 1896.

Father: Adrian Lewis.

Mother: Sarah Lewis (nee Broome).

Father's Occupation: Moulder and Fitter.

Education: Milford Haven National School.

Pre-Service Employment: Fish Packer at Milford Haven.

Service Record: Enlisted 11th Welch Regiment, 4th September, 1914 (Service No. 16224); served France, 6th September, 1915-16th October, 1915; served Salonika, 8th November, 1915-end of hostilies (wounded twice); discharged, 16th April, 1919; served as a Sergeant in the Milford Haven Home Guard during the Second World War.

Rewards, Decorations and Medals: Victoria Cross (for action at Macukovo, near Seres, Salonika, 22nd/23rd October, 1916); 1914-15 Star; British War Medal; Victory Medal; Defence Medal; Coronation Medal (1937); Coronation Medal (1953); Medaille Militaire (France, L.G. 1st May, 1917); Commander in Chief's Certificate for Good Service (1st January, 1945).

Post-Service Employment: Ice Foreman, Milford Haven Fishmarket.

Married: Edith Etherington at Haverfordwest, Pembrokeshire, 9th October, 1920.

Children: Three sons.

Died: 22nd February, 1977, at his home, 26 Prioryville, Milford Haven, Pembrokeshire.

Buried: 25th February, 1977, at Milford Cemetery, Milford Haven.

Memorials: Milford Cemetery, Milford Haven; Haverfordwest War Memorial (as having been unveiled by him); Milford Haven Museum.

Location of VC: Held by the family.

Citation for VC: L.G. 15th December, 1916.

"For most conspicuous bravery and devotion to duty during a raid. On reaching the enemy trenches, Private Lewis was twice wounded but refused to be attended to, and showed great gallantry in searching enemy dugouts. He was again wounded and again refused attendance. At this point three of the enemy were observed to be approaching and Private Lewis immediately attacked them, single handed, capturing all. Subsequently, during the retirement he went to the assistance of a wounded man, and under heavy shell and rifle fire, brought him to our lines, on reaching which he collapsed. Private Lewis showed throughout a brilliant example of courage, endurance and devotion to duty."

He was decorated with the VC by H.M. King George V at Buckingham Palace, 5th February, 1917.

SERGEANT ALBERT WHITE
2nd South Wales Borderers

Full Name: Albert White.

Place of Birth: Not known. The family are believed to have resided at 54 Lamb Street, Kirkdale, Liverpool, and this may have been his birthplace.

Date of Birth: Not known. He is generally regarded as having been born in 1896 but his age on enlistment would suggest that he was born circa. 1889.

Father: Thomas (or James) White.

Mother: Susan White (nee Percival).

Father's Occupation: Ship's Carpenter.

Education: Everton Terrace School, Liverpool.

Pre-Service Employment: Merchant Seaman.

Service Record: Enlisted in the Royal Army Medical Corps at Liverpool, 23rd October, 1914 (aged 24 years 330 days); transferred to the South Wales Borderers, 1st June, 1915 (Service No. 24866); served with the Mediterranean Expeditionary Force, 30th June, 1915-16th March, 1916 (present in Gallipoli and Egypt); served Western Front, March, 1916-10th January, 1917; Sergeant, 2nd July, 1916; served Western Front, 17th April, 1917-19th May, 1917.

Rewards, Decorations and Medals: Victoria Cross (for action at Monchy-le-Preux, France, 19th May, 1917); 1914-15 Star; British War Medal; Victory Medal.

Married: Details not known.

Children: None recorded.

Died: K. in A. Monchy-le-Preux, France, during the Battle of Arras, 19th May, 1917.

Buried: No known grave.

Memorials: Arras Memorial, France, Bay 6.

Location of VC: Held by family.

Citation for VC: L.G. 27th June, 1917.

"For most conspicuous bravery and devotion to duty. Realising, during an attack, that one of the enemy's machine guns, which had previously been located, would hold up the whole advance of his company, Sergeant White, without the slightest hesitation and regardless of all personal danger, dashed ahead of his company to capture the gun. When within a few yards of the gun, he fell riddled with bullets, having thus willingly sacrificed his life in order that he might secure the success of the operations and the welfare of his comrades."

The VC was presented to his father by H.M. King George V at Buckingham Palace, 21st July, 1917.

SEAMAN WILLIAM WILLIAMS
R.N.R. HMS Pargust

Full Name: William Williams.

Place of Birth: 6 Well Street, Amlwch Port, Anglesey.

Date of Birth: 5th October, 1890.

Father: Richard Williams.

Mother: Ann Williams.

Father's Occupation: Believed to have been a longshoreman and fisherman at Amlwch Port.

Education: Amlwch Port School.

Pre-Service Employment: Served aboard the Beaumaris schooner 'Meyric', sailing on three voyages to the Rio Grande, South America.

Service Record: Enlisted in the Royal Naval Reserve as a Seaman/Gunner, 29th September, 1914 (Service No. 6224A); mobilised for service, 2nd October, 1914; served HMS Farnborough (Q-Ship), 1917; served HMS Pargust (Q-Ship), 1917, wounded; served HMS Dunraven (Q-Ship), 1917; served HMS Eilian; discharged from RNR, 6th November, 1918, as medically unfit !or further service with the rank of Leading Seaman; involved in the sinking of U-83 (17th February, 1917), UC.29 (7th June, 1917) and in the action against UC.79 (8th August, 1917).

Rewards, Decorations and Medals: Victoria Cross (for action aboard HMS Pargust, 7th June, 1917); Distinguished Service Medal (for action aboard HMS Farnborough, 17th February, 1917); Bar to Distinguished Service Medal (for action aboard HMS Dunraven, 8th August, 1917, L.G. 2nd November, 1917); 1914-15 Star; British War Medal; Victory Medal; Defence Medal; Coronation Medal (1937); Coronation Medal (1953); Medaille Militaire (France, for action aboard HMS Pargust, 7th June, 1917); Gold watch and illuminated address from the town of Amlwch, £150 of War Bonds from the County of Anglesey.

Post-Service Employment: Shoreworker, LNER Docks, Holyhead, Anglesey. It is believed that he did try to set up a coal merchant business in Holyhead between the wars, Founder member of the Holyhead Branch of the British Legion (served as their Standard Bearer).

Married: 1) Elizabeth Jane Wright; 2) Mrs. Annie Hanlon (widow).

Children: Believed to have had one daughter and one stepdaughter.

Died: 23rd October, 1965 at his home, 31 Station Road, Holyhead, Anglesey.

Buried: Amlwch Cemetery.

Memorials: Amlwch Cemetery; Royal British Legion Club, Holyhead; William Williams VC Estate, Amlwch Port; Council School, Amlwch Port; Amlwch Sailing Club.

Location of VC: Private Collector, North America.

Citation for VC: L.G. 20th July, 1917.

"Lieutenant Stuart and Seaman Williams were selected by the officers and ship's company respectively of one of H.M. ships to receive the Victoria Cross under Rule 13 of the Royal Warrant dated 29th January, 1856."

This vague citation resulted in the awards becoming known as the "Mystery VCs" (along with those awarded to other members of the Q-Ship service in the Great War) and further details are hereby provided:

On June 7th, 1917, HMS Pargust (a converted tramp steamer of about 3,000 tons) was searching for German U-Boats south of Ireland. At 8 am a torpedo was fired at the ship and struck near the water line damaging the engine-room. The ship's panic party rushed to the boats and began to pull away. At 8.15 am a periscope was spotted on the port side about 400 yards from the ship and moving towards them. The submarine circled for some time, undoubtedly unable to make up its mind as to the nature of the ship and, as the Q-Ship scheme had been discovered by the enemy, the U-Boat commander was determined to find out whether HMS Pargust was a genuine merchant vessel or a decoy. If the latter, he would fire another torpedo and sink her. At 8.33 am, obviously convinced of the ship's innocent purpose, the submarine broke surface and began to move around Pargust's stern. Commander Campbell decided to wait until he could be sure of the best possible angle before opening fire with his concealed guns. As the submarine passed the ship's starboard quarter, Campbell spotted the conning tower hatch was open and continued to hold his fire. At last, at 8.36, Pargust's gun crews received the order to open fire. Taken completely unawares the submarine was a sitting duck. The first shot went straight through the conning tower to be followed by others in quick succession. After a short but savage bombardment, the submarine was heard to explode and sank some 300 yards from Pargust. When the details of the action reached the Admiralty, the ship was nominated for the Victoria Cross under the ballot system which allowed the entire crew to vote for one officer and one man to receive the award on behalf of the ship. The vote was taken and the Cross went to Lieutenant R. N. Stuart, DSO, and Seaman William Williams, DSM. In the words of the ship's commander, Commander Gordon Campbell, VC, " . . . any one man could spoil the show . . . one man could save the show. When the explosion of the torpedo took place, the releasing weight of the starboard gun ports was freed by the force of the explosion, and but for the great presence of mind of Williams in taking the whole weight of the port on himself and so preventing it falling down and prematurely exposing the gun, the action might never have taken place." In carrying out this gallant deed (which lasted for 36 minutes) William Williams received a severe injury to his back which was supporting the considerable weight of the gun-port.

He was decorated with the VC by H.M. King George V at Buckingham Palace, in July, 1917.

CORPORAL JAMES DAVIES
13th Royal Welch Fusiliers

Full Name: James Llewelyn Davies.

Place of Birth: Fronwen, Wyndham, Ogmore Vale, Glamorgan. He later resided at 8 Nantymoel Row, Nantymoel, Glamorgan.

Date of Birth: 16th March, 1886.

Father: John Davies.

Mother: Martha Davies.

Father's Occupation: Collier/Steelworker.

Education: Ogmore Vale and Nantymoel Formal Education Council Schools.

Pre-Service Employment: Collier, Wyndham Colliery, Ogmore Vale. He was a member of the South Wales Miners Federation.

Service Record: Enlisted in Royal Garrison Artillery at Bridgend, Glamorgan, 12th October, 1914 (Service No. 44304); transferred to Royal Welch Fusiliers, 5th June, 1915 (Service No. 31161); served in the Dardanelles operations until December, 1915, when he was hospitalised at Alexandria, Egypt, suffering from enteric fever; returned to Britain January, 1916 and treated at Stobhill Military Hospital, Scotland; rejoined Royal Welch Fusiliers, October, 1916; dates of promotions not known; served France and Flanders, October, 1916-July, 1917.

Rewards, Decorations and Medals: Victoria Cross (for action at Polygon Wood, Pilkem, Belgium, 30th July, 1917); 1914-15 Star; British War Medal; Victory Medal.

Married: Elizabeth Ann, daughter of Mr. William Richards, 5 Llewelyn Street, Nantymoel, 24th March, 1906. She later remarried becoming Mrs. Derby.

Children: Three sons and one daughter.

Died: Died of wounds received at Pilkem, Belgium, 31st July, 1917.

Buried: Canada Farm Cemetery, Elverdinghe, Belgium, Plot 2, Row B, Grave 18.

Memorials: Canada Farm Cemetery, Belgium; Nantymoel War Memorial, Glamorgan; Berwyn Centre, Nantymoel; Poem 'Elegy' by Mogg Williams.

Location of VC: Royal Welch Fusiliers Museum, Caernarfon Castle, Caernarfon.

Citation for VC: L.G. 6th September, 1917.

"For most conspicuous bravery during an attack on the enemy line, this non-commissioned officer pushed through our own barrage and, single handed, attacked a machine gun emplacement after serveral men had been killed in attempting to take it. He bayonetted one of the machine gun crew and brought in another man, together with a captured gun.

"Corporal Davies, although wounded, then led a bombing party to the assault of a defended house, and killed a sniper who was harrassing his platoon. This gallant non-commissioned officer has since died of wounds received during the attack."

The VC was presented to his widow and eldest son by H.M. King George V at Buckingham Palace, 20th October, 1917.

SERGEANT ROBERT BYE
1st Welsh Guards

Full Name: Robert James Bye.

Place of Birth: 13 Maritime Street, Pontypridd. The family later moved to 21 Woodfield Street, Penrhiwceibr.

Date of Birth: 12th December, 1889.

Father: Martin Bye.

Mother: Sarah Jane Bye (nee Edwards).

Father's Occupation: Collier.

Education: Penrhiwceibr School.

Pre-Service Employment: Collier at Deep Duffryn Colliery, Mountain Ash and other local mines.

Service Record: Enlisted Welsh Guards, 3rd April, 1915 (Service No. 939); Lance Corporal, 13th March, 1916; Corporal, 21st September, 1916; Sergeant, 4th April, 1917; served France and Flanders; discharged 1st February, 1919; re-enlisted Notts and Derby Regiment, 21st August, 1919; discharged c. 1925; re-enlisted in the Sherwood Forresters during the Second World War as a Sergeant Major.

Rewards, Decorations and Medals: Victoria Cross (for action during the Third Battle of Ypres, Woods 15 and 16 and at the Yser Canal, 31st July, 1917); 1914-15 Star; British War Medal; Victory Medal; Coronation Medal (1937); Coronation Medal (1953).

Post-Service Employment: Collier at Warsop Main, Firbeck and Wellbeck Collieries, Nottinghamshire. Also worked as a Temporary Police Constable at Mansfield.

Married: Mabel Lloyd of Penrhiwceibr (formerly Aberfan) at Pontypridd, 14th October, 1912.

Children: Two sons and two daughters.

Died: 23rd August, 1962 at his daughter's home, 49 Hammerwater Drive, Warsop, near Mansfield, Nottinghamshire. His address at the time was 120a Sherwood Street, Warsop.

Buried: Warsop Cemetery, Warsop, Nottinghamshire, 28th August, 1962.

Memorials: Warsop Cemetery; Guards Chapel, Roll of Honour, Wellington Barracks, London.

Location of VC: Welsh Guards.

Citation for VC: L.G. 6th September, 1917.

"For most conspicuous bravery. Sergeant Bye displayed the utmost courage and devotion to duty during an attack on the enemy's position. Seeing that the leading waves were being troubled by two enemy block-houses, he, on his own initiative, rushed at one of them and put the garrison out of action. He then rejoined his company and went forward to the assault of the second objective.

"When the troops had gone forward to the attack on the third objective a party was detailed to clear up a line of blockhouses which had been passed. Sergeant Bye volunteered to take charge of this party, accomplished his object and took many prisoners. He subsequently advanced to the third objective, capturing a number of prisoners, thus rendering invaluable assistance to the assaulting companies.

"He displayed throughout the most remarkable initiative."

N.B. During the action, Sergeant Bye killed, wounded or captured over seventy of the enemy.

He was decorated with the VC by H.M. King George V at Buckingham Palace, 26th September, 1917.

SERGEANT IVOR REES
11th South Wales Borderers

Full Name: Ivor Rees.

Place of Birth: Union Street, Felinfoel, Llanelli, Carmarthenshire. The family later moved to 18 Long Row, Felinfoel.

Date of Birth: 18th October, 1893.

Father: David Rees.

Mother: Ann Rees (nee Bowen).

Father's Occupation: Electrical Engineer.

Education: Pwll Llanelli Rural School.

Pre-Service Employment: Steelworker at Llanelli Steelworks.

Service Record: Enlisted South Wales Borderers, 9th November, 1914 (Service No. 20002); posted overseas 4th December, 1915; Lance Corporal, 5th August, 1915; Corporal, 1st December, 1915; Sergeant, 19th September, 1916; CSM, 5th September, 1917; returned to Britain, 11th February, 1918; discharged, 31st March, 1921; re-enlisted 4th Welch Regiment (Territorial Force); discharged 30th December, 1921; served as CSM to the 2nd Carmarthenshire Home Guard during the Second World War.

Rewards, Decorations and Medals: Victoria Cross (for action at Pilkem, Belgium, 31st July, 1917); 1914-15 Star; British War Medal; Victory Medal; Defence Medal; Coronation Medal (1937); Coronation Medal (1953); Victory Medal (USA issue, clasps for Meuse-Argonne, Aisne-Marne, Defensive Sector). He also received an illuminated address from the villagers of Pwll, Llanelli.

Post-Service Employment: Unemployed for two years after the Great War then employed by Llanelli Borough Council as a Water Inspector and Cleansing Superintendent until his retirement in 1959.

Married: Martha, daughter of Evan and Sarah Jenkins of Llanelli (formerly of Towyn, Merioneth), 30th September, 1917.

Children: Two sons and three daughters.

Died: 11th March, 1967, at his home, 5 Craddock Street, Llanelli.

Buried: Cremated.

Memorials: None known.

Location of VC: South Wales Borderers Museum, Brecon.

Citation for VC: L.G. 14th September, 1917.

"For most conspicuous bravery in attack. A hostile machine-gun opened fire at close range, inflicting many casualties. Leading his platoon forward by short rushes, Sergeant Rees gradually worked his way round the right flank to the rear of the gun position. When he was about twenty yards from the machine-gun he rushed forward towards the team, shot one and bayonetted another. He then bombed the large concrete emplacement killing five and capturing thirty prisoners of whom two were officers, in addition to an undamaged gun."

He was decorated with the VC by H.M. King George V at Buckingham Palace, 26th September, 1917.

2nd LIEUTENANT FREDERICK BIRKS
6th Australian Imperial Force

Full Name: Frederick Birks.

Place of Birth: Lane End, Buckley, Flintshire.

Date of Birth: 31st August, 1894.

Father: Samuel Birks.

Mother: Mary Birks (nee Williams).

Father's Occupation: Groom/Collier.

Education: St. Matthew's Church School, Buckley, Flintshire.

Pre-Service Employment: Apprentice at the Annealing Plant, John Summer's Steelworks, Shotton. He emigrated to Australia where he was employed as a waiter in Melbourne whilst staying with relatives.

Service Record: Enlisted Australian Imperial Force, 1st Division, 18th August, 1914; assigned to 2nd Field Ambulance Unit, 2nd Infantry Brigade; served Gallipoli, 1915; wounded 20th June, 1915; Lance Corporal, April, 1916; served France and Flanders, March 1916-September, 1917; Corporal, August, 1916; believed to have been promoted to Sergeant late 1916; commissioned 2nd Lieutenant, 6th (Victoria) Australian Infantry Force, 26th April, 1917.

Rewards, Decorations and Medals: Victoria Cross (for action during the Third Battle of Ypres, 20th September, 1917); Military Medal (for action at Porzieres, July, 1916); 1914-15 Star; British War Medal; Victory Medal.

Married: Not married.

Children: None.

Died: K. in A. Red Line, Glencourse Wood, 3rd Battle of Ypres, 21st September, 1917.

Buried: North Perth Cemetery, Zillebeke, Belgium, Plot 1, Row G, Grave 45.

Memorials: North Perth Cemetery, Zillebeke, Belgium; Australian War Memorial, Canberra, Australia; Buckley Churchyard, Buckley, Flintshire; Royal British Legion Club, Buckley, Flintshire.

Location of VC: Australian War Memorials, Hall of Valour, Canberra, Australia.

Citation for VC: L.G. 8th November, 1917.

"For most conspicuous bravery in attack when, accompanied by only a corporal, he rushed a strong point which was holding up the advance. The corporal was wounded by a bomb, but Second Lieutenant Birks went on by himself, killed the remainder of the enemy occupying the position and captured a machine gun. Shortly afterwards he organised a small party and attacked another strong point which was occupied by about twenty-five of the enemy, of whom many were killed and an officer and fifteen men captured. During the consolidation this officer did magnificent work in reorganising parties of other units which had been disorganised during the operations. By his wonderful coolness and personal bravery Second Lieutenant Birks kept his men in splendid spirits throughout. He was killed at his post by a shell whilst endeavouring to extricate some of his men who had been buried by a shell."

The VC was presented to his brother, Sergeant Samuel Birks, RFA, by H.M. King George V at Buckingham Palace, 19th December, 1917.

ACTING LIEUTENANT COLONEL LEWIS EVANS
The Black Watch, Commanding 1st Lincolnshire Regiment

Full Name: Lewis Pugh Evans.

Place of Birth: Lovesgrove, Abermadd, Aberystwyth, Cardiganshire.

Date of Birth: 3rd January, 1881.

Father: Sir Griffith Pugh Evans, K.C.I.E., D.L., J.P.

Mother: Lady Emelia Savi Evans (nee Hills)

Father's Occupation: Barrister at Law.

Education: Eton College, January, 1895-December, 1898; RMA Sandhurst, January-December, 1899.

Service Record: Commissioned 2nd Lieutenant, The Black Watch, 23rd December, 1899; served South Africa, 1899-1902 (present at actions at Polar Grove, Dreifontein, Vet River, February-May, 1900; Johannesburg, Pretoria and Diamond Hill, May-June, 1900; Belfast, Orange River Colony, July, 1900-January, 1902); Lieutenant, 1st May, 1901; Captain, 27th October, 1906; Staff College, 1914; GSO 3 War Office, 1914; attached No. 3 Squadron, Royal Flying Corps as Observer, 22nd September, 1914-13th December, 1914 (qualifed as a pilot); Company Commander, Black Watch, 13th December, 1914-1st May, 1915; Major, 1st September, 1915; Brigade Major, 7th Infantry Brigade, 3rd Division; Acting Lieutenant Colonel, 1st Lincolnshire Regiment, 23rd March, 1917-4th October, 1917 (wounded); Acting Lieutenant Colonel, 1st Black Watch, 23rd January, 1918-9th June, 1918; Temporary Brigadier General, 14th Infantry Brigade, 32nd Division, 10th June, 1918-7th February, 1919; Temporary Brigadier General, Base Commandant, Rhine Army at Rotterdam, 8th February, 1919-5th November, 1919; Temporary Lieutenant Colonel, Instructor Senior Officers' School (Class Z and Y), 18th January, 1920-23rd May, 1921; Brigade Major, 7th June, 1921; GSO 2, 16th February, 1923; Lieutenant Colonel, commanding 2nd Black Watch, 15th September, 1926; Brevet Colonel, 1st January, 1928; Colonel, 5th September, 1930; AAG, Eastern Command, 15th May, 1931; Brigadier, commanding 159th (Welsh Border) Infantry Brigade (Territorial Army), 18th May, 1933-7th May, 1937; half-pay, 18th May, 1937; retired, 3rd January, 1938; Military Liaison Officer, Wales Region HQ, 1939-41; served as Chairman of one of the selection boards for granting commissions in the Home Guard, December, 1940.

Rewards, Decorations and Medals: Victoria Cross (for action near Zonnebeke, Belgium, 4th October, 1917); CB (L.G. 9th June, 1938); CMG (L.G. 3rd June, 1919); DSO (for action at Hooge, 16th June, 1915); Bar to DSO (for action at Givenchy, April, 1918); Order of St. John; Queen's South Africa Medal (clasps for Dreifontein, Johannesburg, Belfast, Diamond Hill, Cape Colony); King's South Africa Medal; 1914 Star (with clasp); British War Medal; Victory Medal (M. in D.); Defence Medal; British War Medal (1939-45); Coronation Medal (1911); Jubilee Medal (1935); Coronation Medal (1937); Coronation Medal (1953); Croix de Guerre (France); Order of Leopold (Belgium); Deputy Lieutenant of Cardiganshire (1937-62).

Post-Service Employment: Retired Brigadier. Landowner.

Married: Margaret Dorothea Seagrave, daughter of John Carbery Pryce-Rice and Dame Margaret Pryce-Rice of Llwyn Y Brain, Llandovery, Carmarthenshire, 6th October, 1918, at Holy Trinity Church, Sloane Square, London. She was killed in a railway accident in Devon in 1921.

Children: One son.

Died: Paddington Station, London, 30th November, 1962 (of a heart attack).

Buried: Llanbadarn Churchyard, Cardiganshire.

Memorials: Llanbadarn Churchyard, Cardiganshire.

Location of VC: Held by the family.

Citation for VC: L.G. 26th November, 1917.
"For most conspicuous bravery and leadership. Lieutenant Colonel Evans took his battalion, in perfect order, through a terrific enemy barrage, personally formed up all units and led them to the assault. While a strong

machine gun emplacement was causing casualties, and the troops were working round the flank, Lieutenant Colonel Evans rushed at it himself, and by firing his revolver through the loophole, forced the garrison to capitulate. After capturing the first objective, he was severely wounded in the shoulder, but refused to be bandaged, and reformed the troops, pointed out all future objectives and again led his battalion forward. Again badly wounded, he nevertheless continued to command until the second objective was won, and after consolidation, collapsed from loss of blood. As there were numerous casualties, he refused assistance, and by his own efforts ultimately reached the dressing station.

"His example of cool bravery stimulated in all ranks the highest valour and determination to win."

He was decorated with the VC by H.M. King George V at Buckingham Palace, 2nd January, 1918.

Citation for DSO: L.G. 24th July, 1915.

"For conspicuous gallantry and devotion to duty on June 16th, 1915, at Hooge, when, after troops had become much mixed up, he continually moved up and down the firing line under heavy fire from 10 a.m. till midnight reorganising units and bringing back their reports."

Citation for Bar to DSO: L.G. 16th September, 1918.

"For conspicuous gallantry and devotion to duty in a three days' battle. On the first day he was moving about everywhere in his forward area directing operations, the next day he personally conducted a reconnaissance for a counter-attack, which was carried out on the third day. It was largely due to his untiring energy and method that the enemy were checked and finally driven out of our forward system."

N.B. Lewis Pugh Evans was the great-nephew of Sir James Hills-Johnes, VC, and the nephew of Lt. William Cubitt, VC. He was a pall-bearer at the funeral of King George V.

ACTING CORPORAL JOHN COLLINS
25th Royal Welsh Fusiliers

Full Name: John Collins.

Place of Birth: Taunton or West Hatch, Somerset. His family moved to Merthyr when he was about 10 years of age where they resided at 54 High Street, Penydarren.

Date of Birth: 10th September, 1877.

Father: Thomas Collins.

Mother: Mary Ann Collins.

Father's Occupation: Collier.

Education: West Hatch Village School, Somerset.

Pre-Service Employment: Details not known but was probably employed in the mining industry.

Service Record: Enlisted Royal Horse Artillery as a Driver, 18th November, 1895 (Service No. 12118); served in South Africa during the Boer War (was one of the first troops to enter Ladysmith with the relief column); served India; discharged, date unknown; enlisted in The Welsh Horse (Service No. 340); served Gallipoli, Syria, Palestine, France and Flanders during the Great War; Welsh Horse absorbed into 25th Royal Welsh Fusiliers, 4th

March, 1917; Sergeant, 31st October, 1917; wounded, France, 8th October, 1917; discharged 20th February, 1919; served as Sergeant Major in the Home Guard at Dowlais, 15th August, 1940-20th September, 1942.

Rewards, Decorations and Medals: Victoria Cross (for action at Wadi Saba, Beersheba, Palestine, 31st October, 1917); Distinguished Conduct Medal (L.G. 1st May, 1918); Queen's South Africa Medal (clasps for Belfast, Diamond Hill, Johannesburg, Orange Free State, Cape Colony); King's South Africa Medal (clasps for South Africa 1901 and South Africa 1902); 1914-15 Star; British War Medal; Victory Medal; Coronation Medal (1937).

Post-Service Employment: Collier, Bedliniog Colliery, Penydarren, Glamorgan, between the Boer War and the Great War; Tip Labourer, Dowlais and Merthyr Tydfil; Security Guard at Dowlais Steelworks.

Married: Mary Ellen, daughter of John and Mary O'Brian, St. Illtyd's R.C. Church, Dowlais, 1910. They lived at 21 Caerhendy Street, Penydarren, Merthyr Tydfil.

Children: Six sons and two daughters.

Died: 3rd September, 1951, at St. Tydfil's Hospital, Merthyr Tydfil.

Buried: Pant Cemetery, Merthyr Tydfil, Roman Catholic Section, 8th September, 1951. The funeral service was delayed by an overtime ban by the grave diggers which prevented many mourners from attending.

Memorials: Pant Cemetery, Merthyr Tydfil; Collins Court, Wrexham.

Location of VC: Royal Welch Fusiliers Museum, Carenarfon Castle, Caernarfon.

Citation for VC: L.G. 18th December, 1917.
"For most conspicuous bravery, resource and leadership when, after deployment, prior to an attack, his battalion was forced to lie out in the open under heavy shell and machine-gun fire which caused many casualties. This gallant non-commissioned officer repeatedly went out under heavy fire and brought wounded back to cover, thus saving many lives.
"In subsequent operations throughout the day, Corporal Collins was conspicuous in rallying and leading his command. He led the final assault with the utmost skill in spite of heavy fire at close range and uncut wire. He bayonetted fifteen of the enemy and, with a Lewis gun section, pressed on beyond the objective and covered the reorganisation and consolidation most effectively although isolated and under fire from snipers and guns.
"He showed throughout a magnificent example of initiative and fearlessness."

He was decorated with the VC by H.M. King George V at Buckingham Palace, 1st June, 1918.

Citation for DCM: L.G. 1st May, 1918.
"For conspicuous gallantry and devotion to duty. As soon as the enemy opened fire at point blank range, he rallied all the men near him, took control of a portion of the line, and brought every available rifle to bear on the enemy.
"During the consolidation he did exceptionally good work, and later, when the enemy counter-attacked, went under heavy fire from post to post to see that they were being held to the best advantage. His ability and devotion to duty were of the highest order."

CAPTAIN JOHN FOX RUSSELL
Royal Army Medical Corps

Full Name: John Fox Russell.

Place of Birth: Plas Tanalltran, Holyhead, Anglesey. The family later moved to 5 Victoria Terrace, Holyhead, Anglesey.

Date of Birth: 27th January, 1893.

Father: Dr. William Fox Russell.

Mother: Ethel Maria Fox Russell (nee Thornbury).

Father's Occupation: General Practitioner in Holyhead. He was also an officer in the 6th Royal Welch Fusiliers (Territorial Force).

Education: Holyhead County School; passed the entrance examination for a choristership at Magdalen College School in 1904 but left when his voice broke in 1907; St. Bees School, Cumberland, 1908-09 (served in the OTC); passed entrance examination for Royal College of Surgeons, Dublin, but attended the Medical School at the Middlesex Hospital, London, instead, commencing in October, 1909 (served in the London University OTC).

Service Record: Commissioned 2nd Lieutenant, Royal Welsh Fusiliers Territorial Force, 5th December, 1913; Lieutenant, 6th (Anglesey and Carnarvonshire) Battalion, Royal Welsh Fusiliers, 2nd September, 1914; Captain, 27th January, 1915; as his battalion had not been sent overseas he applied to the War Office for permission to continue his medical studies and returned to the Middlesex Hospital where he was awarded the Diploma of the Society of Apothecaries in March, 1916; transferred to the Royal Army Medical Corps; attached to the Royal Field Artillery in France, 10th October, 1916; transferred, at his own request, to serve as Medical Officer to 6th Royal Welch Fusiliers in Egypt; served in Palestine, 1917.

Rewards, Decorations and Medals: Victoria Cross (for action at Tel-el-Khuweilfeh, Palestine, 6th November, 1917); Military Cross (for action at the First Battle of Gaza, Palestine, 1917); British War Medal; Victory Medal; Territorial War Medal.

Married: 23rd September, 1916, to Alma G. Taylor, at St. Mark's Church, Tunbridge Wells (she later re-married twice becoming Mrs. Whitehouse and Mrs. Thomas, and resided in New Zealand).

Children: None.

Died: K. in A. at Tel-el-Khuweilfeh, Palestine, 6th November, 1917.

Buried: Near Tel-el-Khuweilfeh, Palestine, then re-interred at Beersheba War Cemetery, Palestine, Plot F, Grave 31.

Memorials: Beersheba War Cemetery, Palestine; St. Bees School, Cumberland; Chapel Cloisters, Magdalen College, Oxford; Holyhead War Memorial; Royal British Legion Club, Holyhead; Aldeburgh Church, Suffolk; Students' Common Room, Middlesex Hospital, London; 5 Victoria Terrace, Holyhead; RAMC Headquarters, Millbank, London; County Secondary School, Holyhead; Dr. John Fox Russell, VC, Scholarship, Holyhead.

Location of VC: Royal Army Medical Corps Museum, Aldershot.

Citation for VC: L.G. 11th January, 1918.

"For most conspicuous bravery displayed in action until he was killed. Captain Russell repeatedly went out to attend to the wounded under murderous fire from snipers and machine guns, and in many cases where no other means were at hand carried them in himself although almost exhausted. He showed the highest possible degree of valour."

The VC was presented to his widow by H.M. King George V at Buckingham Palace, 2nd March, 1918.

Citation for MC: L.G. 16th August, 1917.

"For conspicuous gallantry and devotion to duty. He showed the greatest courage and skill in collecting wounded of all regiments, and in dressing them, under continuous shell and rifle fire."

CAPTAIN RICHARD WAIN
17th Manchester Regiment attached 1st Tank Corps

Full Name: Richard William Leslie Wain.

Place of Birth: 4 Victoria Square, Penarth, Glamorgan. The family later moved to Woodside, The Avenue, Llandaff, Glamorgan.

Date of Birth: 5th December, 1896.

Father: Harris Wain.

Mother: Florence Emily Wain, daughter of William Tucker of Abergavenny, Monmouthshire.

Father's Occupation: Solicitor at Llandaff.

Education: Llandaff Cathedral School, Llandaff; St. Bees School, Cumberland, 1911-14 (passed Higher Certificate Oxford & Cambridge Joint Board, OTC, Holder of House Scholarship); intended to go to Oxford University.

Service Record: Enlisted 7th (Cyclist) Battalion, The Welch Regiment, September, 1914; transferred to Manchester Regiment (Public Schools Battalion), December, 1914; commissioned 2nd Lieutenant, 16th July, 1915; served France and Flanders, March, 1916-November, 1917; Temporary Lieutenant, 12th July, 1916; transferred to Tank Corps, 2nd January, 1917; fought in the Tank Corps at the Somme, 1st July, 1916 (wounded); wounded 22nd September, 1917; fought at the Battle of Cambrai, 20th November, 1917; Acting Captain, 12th November, 1916.

Rewards, Decorations and Medals: Victoria Cross (for action at Marcoing, near Cambrai, 20th November, 1917); British War Medal; Victory Medal.

Married: Not married.

Children: None.

Died: K. in A. Marcoing, near Cambrai, 20th November, 1917.

Buried: Next to his tank, Abu-Ben-Adam II, on the Hindenburg Line near Marcoing. Site of grave not recorded.

Memorials: Cambrai Memorial, France; Louveral Military Cemetery; St. Bees School, Cumberland; Llandaff Cathedral, Llandaff, Glamorgan.

Location of VC: Not known.

Citation for VC: L.G. 13th February, 1918.

"For most conspicuous bravery in command of a section of Tanks. During an attack the Tank in which he was, was disabled by a direct hit near an enemy strong point which was holding up the attack. Captain Wain and one man, both seriously wounded, were the only survivors. Though bleeding profusely from his wounds, he refused the attention of stretcher bearers, rushed from behind the Tank with a Lewis gun, and captured the strong point, taking about half the garrison prisoners. Although his wounds were very serious he picked up a rifle and continued to fire at the retiring enemy until he received a fatal wound in the head. It was due to the valour displayed by Captain Wain that the infantry were able to advance."

The VC was presented to his parents by H.M. King George V at Buckingham Palace, 20th April, 1918.

ACTING CAPTAIN ARTHUR LASCELLES
3rd Durham Light Infantry

Full Name: Arthur Moore Lascelles.

Place of Birth: Wilby Lodge, Nightingale Lane, Streatham, London. His home address was Penmaen, Pennel, Machynlleth, Merionethshire.

Date of Birth: 12th October, 1880.

Father: John Lascelles.

Mother: Mary Elizabeth Lascelles (nee Cotton).

Father's Occupation: Gentleman.

Education: Malvern School; Uppingham School, May, 1895-December, 1898 (House XV and XI); University College of North Wales, Bangor, 1899; Edinburgh University, 1899.

Pre-Service Employment: Emigrated to South Africa in 1902 and was employed as a professional soldier.

Service Record: Enlisted as a Trooper, Cape Mounted Rifles, 11th August, 1902; transferred to 1st South African Mounted Riflemen, 1st April, 1913; served De Wet Rebellion, 1914; served South West African Campaign, 1914-15; discharged as Quarter-Master Sergeant, 10th October, 1915; returned to Britain; commissioned 3rd Durham Light Infantry, 23rd December, 1915; attended Officers' Training Course at Cambridge, 1st January-3rd February, 1916; attended sniping course at Rugby, July, 1916; served France and Flanders attached 14th Durham Light Infantry, July-September, 1916; wounded by shrapnel, Somme, 18th September, 1916, invalided to England; served France and Flanders, 11th Durham Light Infantry, February-May, 1917; transferred to 14th Durham Light Infantry, May, 1917 and served with them on the Western Front until being wounded severely in the head and right arm (which he lost the further use of) and invalided home in December, 1917; joined 3rd Durham Light Infantry, Western Front, August 1918; Lieutenant, 1st July, 1917; Acting Captain, 20th July, 1917.

Rewards, Decorations and Medals: Victoria Cross (for action at Masnieres, France, 3rd December, 1917); Military Cross (for action near Loos, France, 15th June, 1917); 1914-15 Star (South African Issue); British War Medal; Victory Medal.

Married: 7th December, 1907, Sophia Hardiman at Idutywa, Transkei, South Africa. During the Great War she worked in the canteen of a Midlands munitions factory.

Children: One son.

Died: K. in A. Limont, Fontaine, France, 7th November, 1918. His home address at that time was 9 Richmond Road, Olton, Warwickshire.

Buried: Dourlers Communal Cemetery Extension, France, Plot 2, Row G, Grave 24.

Memorials: Pennel Parish Church, Merionethshire; Pennel War Memorial; University College of North Wales War Memorial; Edinburgh University War Memorial.

Location of VC: Durham Light Infantry Museum.

Citation for VC: L.G. 11th January, 1918.

"For most conspicuous bravery, initiative and devotion to duty when in command of his company in a very exposed position. After a very heavy bombardment, during which Captain Lascelles was wounded, the enemy attacked in strong force but was driven off, success being due to a great degree to the fine example set by this officer, who, refusing to allow his wound to be dressed, continued to encourage his men and organise the defence.

"Shortly afterwards the enemy again attacked and captured the trench, taking several of his men prisoners. Captain Lascelles at once jumped onto the parapet, and, followed by the remainder of his company — twelve men only — rushed across under very heavy machine-gun fire, and drove over sixty of the enemy back, thereby saving a most critical situation. He was untiring in reorganising the position, but shortly afterwards the enemy again attacked and captured the trench and Captain Lascelles, who escaped later. The remarkable determination and gallantry of this officer in the course of operations, during which he received two further wounds, afforded an inspiring example to all."

He was decorated with the VC by H.M. King George V at Buckingham Palace, 23rd March, 1918.

Citation for MC: L.G. 1st January, 1918.

"In the 15 Bis Sector, near Loos, on 15th June, 1917, showed great courage, endurance and initiative in a very successful daylight raid. He commanded a party of forty other ranks. He led then with great gallantry, capturing all his objectives, taking five prisoners and killing twenty Germans. He conducted operations throughout with great coolness and it was largely due to his fine work that the withdrawal of the whole raid was carried out without a casualty. He was the last to leave the trench. The success of the raid was largely due to the valuable reconnaissance carried out by this officer before the raid. This officer has many times been brought to notice for his gallantry in action and has commanded his company very well."

CAPTAIN THOMAS PRYCE
4th Grenadier Guards

Full Name: Thomas Tannatt Pryce.

Place of Birth: The Hague, Holland. The family home was at Pentrehylin Hall, Llandysilio, Montgomeryshire.

Date of Birth: 17th January, 1886.

Father: Thomas Pryce.

Mother: Susannah Pryce (nee Van Motman).

Father's Occupation: Landowner.

Education: Mr. Deede's Preparatory School, Shrewsbury; Shrewsbury School, 1900-1904; Royal Agricultural College, Cirencester, 1905 (two terms).

Pre-Service Employment: Henry Tudor & Son, London. Member of the Stock Exchange, 1913.

Service Record: Enlisted as a Private in The Honourable Artillery Company, 25th August, 1914; served France, December, 1914-November, 1915; commissioned 2nd Lieutenant, 6th Gloucestershire Regiment (Territorial Force), 11th October, 1915; served France, December 1914-November 1915;

wounded during night raid on Gommecourt, 26th November, 1915; invalided home November, 1915; served France, May, 1916-September, 1916; transferred to 4th Grenadier Guards, 11th September, 1916; Lieutenant, 13th September, 1916; served France, February, 1917-April, 1918; Acting Captain, April, 1918.

Rewards, Decorations and Medals: Victoria Cross (for action at Vieux Berquin, France, 11th April, 1918); Military Cross (for action at Gommecourt, 25th/26th November, 1915); Bar to Military Cross (for action, 9th September, 1916); 1914-15 Star; British War Medal; Victory Medal (M. in D.).

Married: Margaret Sybil, daughter of Edward Snow Fordham, Metropolitan Police Magistrate, at Ashwell, Hertfordshire, 11th March, 1908. She later remarried becoming Mrs. Waterall.

Children: Three daughters.

Died: K. in A. at Vieux Berquin, France, 13th April, 1918, following a report that he was missing believed killed. At the time of his death his home address was Craufurd Lodge, Maidenhead (since 1912).

Buried: No known grave.

Memorials: Ploegsteert Memorial, Belgium, Panel 1; War Memorial, Fourcrosses, Llandysilio, Montgomeryshire; Llandysilio Church, Montgomeryshire; Shrewsbury School War Memorial; Stock Exchange War Memorial.

Location of VC: Guards Museum, Wellington Barracks, London (on loan).

Citation for VC: L.G. 22nd May, 1918.

"For most conspicuous bravery, devotion to duty and self sacrifice when in command of a flank on the left of the Grenadier Guards. Having been ordered to attack a village, he personally led forward two platoons, working from house to house, killing some thirty of the enemy, seven of whom he killed himself.

"The next day he was occupying a position with some thirty to forty men, the remainder of his company having become casualties. As early at 8.15 a.m. his left flank was surrounded and the enemy were enfilading him. He was attacked no less than four times during the day and each time beat off the hostile attack, killing many of the enemy. Meanwhile the enemy brought up three field guns to within 300 yards of his line, and were firing over open sights and knocking his trench in. At 6.15 p.m. the enemy had worked to within sixty yards of his trench. He then called on his men, telling them to cheer, and charge the enemy and fight to the last. Led by Captain Pryce they left their trench and drove back the enemy with the bayonet some 100 yards. Half an hour later the enemy had again approached in stronger force. By this time Captain Pryce had only seventeen men left and every round of his ammunition had been fired. Determined that there should be no surrender, he once again led his men in a bayonet charge, and was last seen engaged in a fierce hand-to-hand struggle with overwhelming numbers of the enemy.

"With some forty men he held back at least one enemy battalion for over ten hours. His company undoubtedly stopped the advance through the British line, and thus had great influence on the battle."

The VC was presented to his widow by H.M. King George V at Buckingham Palace, 13th April, 1919.

Citation for MC: L.G. 23rd December, 1915.

"For conspicuous gallantry at Gommecourt on the night of 25th/26th November, 1915. When in charge of an assaulting column he succeeded in entering the German trenches unobserved, clearing them, and bombing large parties of the enemy, who were crowded in deep dug-outs. Although wounded himself, he subsequently extracted his men successfully in face of superior numbers."

Citation for Bar to MC: L.G. 19th July, 1916.

"For conspicuous gallantry in action. He commanded the leading platoon in the assault with great dash and determination, right up to the enemy's trenches, under very heavy fire of all kinds. He set a fine example."

LANCE CORPORAL HENRY WEALE
14th Royal Welch Fusiliers

Full Name: Henry Weale.

Place of Birth: Nine Houses, Shotton, Flintshire. The family later moved to 33 Brook Road, Shotton, Flintshire.

Date of Birth: 2nd October, 1897.

Father: John Weale.

Mother: Sarah Weale (nee Hughes).

Father's Occupation: General Labourer.

Education: St. Ethelwald's School, Shotton, Flintshire.

Pre-Service Employment: Packer at John Summer's Steelworks, Shotton, Flintshire.

Service Record: Enlisted 5th Royal Welch Fusiliers (Territorial Force), 1st November, 1911 (Service No. 915); discharged, 7th September, 1913; enlisted 3rd Royal Welch Fusiliers (Special Reserve), 8th September, 1913 (Service No. 5046); mobilised, 5th August, 1914; served overseas, 1st November, 1914-10th December, 1914 (wounded); served overseas, 16th March, 1915-1st October, 1915 (wounded); served overseas, 14th September, 1916-16th January, 1917 (gassed); served overseas, 22nd August, 1917-28th August, 1918 (wounded); Lance Corporal (unpaid), 26th October, 1917; Lance Corporal, 8th December, 1917; transferred to the Reserve, 16th April, 1919; discharged, 8th September, 1919; re-enlisted, 5th Royal Welch Fusiliers (Territorial Force), 7th February, 1921; served in Ireland; Sergeant, 8th July, 1921; discharged, 6th February, 1922; enlisted Section D Army Reserve, 12th July, 1922; discharged, 12th July, 1926; re-enlisted, National Defence Corps, 25th August, 1939; transferred to Royal Welch Fusiliers and posted to Dover and Salisbury Plain as an airfield guard; discharged as unfit for active service, 29th January, 1941.

Rewards, Decorations and Medals: Victoria Cross (for action at Bazentin-le-Grand, France, 26th August, 1918); 1914 Star; British War Medal; Victory Medal (M. in D.); Defence Medal; British War Medal (1939-45); Coronation Medal (1937); Coronation Medal (1953).

Post-Service Employment: Packer, John Summer's Steelworks, Shotton, Flintshire; Building worker, Melvill, Dunstan & Whitley of Holywell, Flintshire; Road worker, Rhyl Urban District Council. He resided at 22 Prince Edward Road, Rhyl, Flintshire.

Married: Susie, daughter of George Harrison of 5 Hope Place, Rhyl, at St. Ethelwald's Church, Shotton, 16th June, 1919. He moved to live in Rhyl shortly after the wedding.

Children: Four sons and one daughter.

Died: 13th January, 1959, at his son's home in Rhyl.

Buried: Rhyl Cemetery.

Memorials: Rhyl Cemetery, Rhyl, Flintshire; Weale Court, Hightown, Wrexham.

Location of VC: Royal Welch Fusiliers Museum, Caernarfon Castle, Caernarfon.

Citation for VC: L.G. 15th November, 1918.

"For most conspicuous bravery. The adjacent battalion having been held up by enemy machine guns, Lance Corporal Weale was ordered to deal with the hostile posts. When his Lewis gun failed him, on his own initiative, he rushed the nearest posts and killed the crew, then went for the others, the crews of which fled on his approach, this gallant non-commissioned officer pursuing them. His very dashing deed cleared the way for the advance, inspired his comrades and resulted in the capture of all the machine guns."

He was decorated with the VC by H.M. King George V at Buckingham Palace, 1st March, 1919.

CHIEF PETTY OFFICER GEORGE PROWSE
R.N.V.R., Drake Battalion, Royal Naval Division

Full Name: George Prowse.

Place of Birth: Not known but probably Bath or Paulton near Bath, Somerset.

Date of Birth: —

Father: John Prowse.

Mother: —

Father's Occupation: Collier.

Education: —

Pre-Service Employment: Collier at Grovesend Colliery, Swansea, later Mountain Colliery, Gorseinon, Swansea. He lived at various addresses during this time including Station Road, Grovesend (1908) and 22 New Road, Grovesend.

Service Record: Enlisted Royal Naval Volunteer Reserve at Swansea, 25th February, 1915 (Service No. WZ424); Chief Petty Officer, 28th April, 1918; served France and Flanders with Drake Battalion, Royal Naval Division (wounded twice); his service papers have not survived hence the absence of information on his service career.

Rewards, Decorations and Medals: Victoria Cross (for action at Pronville, France, 2nd September, 1918); Distinguished Conduct Medal (for action at Logeast Wood, 21st August, 1918); British War Medal; Victory Medal.

Married: Sarah, daughter of David Lewis, 63 Pentretreharne Road, Landore, at Swansea Registry Office, 8th November, 1913; they lived at 60 Treharne Road, Landore, Swansea.

Children: None.

Died: K. in A. near Arleux, France, during the fighting for the Bapaume — Cambrai Road, 27th September, 1918.

Buried: No known grave.

Memorials: Vis-en-Artois Memorial, France, Panels 1 & 2.

Location of VC: Held by private collector.

Citation for VC: L.G. 30th October, 1918.

"For most conspicuous bravery and devotion to duty when, during an advance, a portion of his company became disorganised by heavy machine gun fire from an enemy strong point. Collecting what men were available he led them with great coolness and bravery against this strong point capturing it together with 23 prisoners and 5 machine guns.

"Later he took a patrol forward in the face of much enemy opposition and established it on important high ground. On another occasion he displayed great heroism by attacking, single handed, an ammunition limber which was trying to recover ammunition, killing three men who accompanied it and capturing the limber.

"Two days later he rendered valuable services when covering the advance of his company with a Lewis gun section, and located later two machine gun positions in a concrete emplacement which were holding up the advance of the battalion on the right. With complete disregard of personal danger he rushed forward and attacked and captured the posts, killing 6 of the enemy and taking 13 prisoners and two machine guns. He was the only survivor of this gallant party but by this daring and heroic action he enabled the battalion on the right to push forward without further machine gun fire from the village. Throughout the whole operation his magnificent example and leadership was an inspiration to all and his courage was superb."

The VC was presented to his widow by H.M. King George V at Buckingham Palace, 17th July, 1919. This was the last VC to be awarded with the blue, Naval ribbon.

Citation for DCM: L.G. 16th January, 1919.

"On 21st August, 1918, at Logeast Wood, he led his men with great gallantry against a machine gun that was holding up the advance of the flank of the company and, in spite of difficulties of heavy mist, he captured it, disposing of the crew. On a subsequent occasion he held a position against repeated counter-attacks which were supported by an intense bombardment for twenty-four hours. His courage, leadership and cheerful disposition had an invaluable effect on his men."

LANCE SERGEANT WILLIAM WARING
25th Royal Welch Fusiliers

Full Name: William Herbert Waring.

Place of Birth: Rock Terrace, Raven Square, Welshpool, Montgomeryshire.

Date of Birth: 13th October, 1885.

Father: Richard Waring.

Mother: Annie Waring (nee Jones).

Father's Occupation: Nailmaker. Formerly a Corporal in the South Wales Borderers. Reputed to have served in the Zulu War in South Africa, 1879. He had lost his left leg.

Education: Christ Church C. of E. Infants School, Welshpool; Boys National School, Berriw Road, Welshpool.

Pre-Service Employment: Employed by Mr. Bushell, poultry dealer, Welshpool.

Service Record: Enlisted in the Montgomeryshire Yeomanry, 1904; Corporal, 23rd May, 1911; Sergeant, 22nd May, 1913; mobilised, 4th August, 1914; in training with 1/1 Montgomeryshire Yeomanry at Cromer; served Egypt and Mesopotamia 16th March, 1916-28th April, 1918; transferred to

25th Royal Welch Fusiliers, 4th March, 1917; reverted to Private at his own request, 21st March, 1917; Acting Sergeant, 31st October, 1917; Acting Company Quarter Master Sergeant, 24th November, 1917; reverted to Private, 29th November, 1917; Corporal, 2nd December, 1917; Acting Sergeant, 7th January, 1918; Sergeant, 9th March, 1918; reverted to Lance Sergeant, 13th April, 1918; served France and Flanders, 7th May, 1918-8th October, 1918.

Rewards, Decorations and Medals: Victoria Cross (for action at Ronssoy, France, 18th September, 1918); Military Medal (L.G. 4th February, 1918); British War Medal; Victory Medal; Territorial Force Efficiency Medal.

Married: Not married.

Children: None.

Died: Died at Le Havre, France, 8th October, 1918, of wounds received in action, 18th September, 1918.

Buried: Sainte Marie Cemetery, Le Havre, Division 62, Plot 5, Row 1, Grave 3.

Memorials: Sainte Marie Cemetery, Le Havre, France; Welshpool War Memorial; Waring Court, Hightown, Wrexham; Waring Court, Alford, Welshpool; name added to his parents' grave at Christ Church, Welshpool.

Location of VC: Welshpool Borough Council.

Citation for VC: L.G. 31st January, 1919.

"For most conspicuous bravery and devotion to duty at Ronssoy on the 18th September, 1918. He led an attack against enemy machine guns which were holding up the advance of neighbouring troops and, in the face of devastating fire from the flank and front, single handed, rushed a strong point, bayonetting four of the garrison and capturing twenty with their guns.

"Lance Sergeant Waring then, under heavy shell and machine gun fire, reorganised his men and led and inspired them for another 400 yards, when he fell mortally wounded.

"His valour, determination and leadership were conspicuous throughout."

The VC was presented to his parents by H.M. King George V at Buckingham Palace, 8th March, 1919.

N.B. Won a silver watch as best shot in his squadron, 1913. Member of the team cup for best Troop. Member of Welshpool Lodge of the Order of Druids. Played soccer for Welshpool, Llanfyllin and Oswestry.

LANCE CORPORAL ALLAN LEWIS
6th Northamptonshire Regiment

Full Name: Leonard Allan Lewis (this is often, incorrectly, recorded as Allan Leonard Lewis).

Place of Birth: Wood Villa, Brilley, Whitney on Wye, Herefordshire.

Date of Birth: 28th February, 1895.

Father: George Lewis.

Mother: Annie Elizabeth Lewis (nee Gidley).

Father's Occupation: Carpenter.

Education: Whitney on Wye School (to the age of thirteen years).

Pre-Service Employment: Farm Labourer; Motor Bus Driver, GWR, Neath to Pontardawe, Glamorgan. At this time he lived at 17 Creswell Road, Neath, Glamorgan.

Service Record: Enlisted R.A.S.C. (Mechanical Transport Section), March, 1915 (Service No. M2/104722); served France, 1915-18; invalided to UK early 1917 with jaundice and hospitalised at Longleat House, Wiltshire; transferred to the Northamptonshire Regiment, date not known (Service No. 58062); served School of Instruction, France; Lance Corporal.

Rewards, Decorations and Medals: Victoria Cross (for action near Lempire, France, 18th/21st September, 1918); 1914-15 Star; British War Medal; Victory Medal.

Married: Not married.

Children: None.

Died: K. in A. (shrapnel wound to the head) at Doleful Post, near Lempire, France, 21st September, 1918.

Buried: 30th September, 1918, near Lempire, France. No known grave. His body was discovered by an Australian soldier who removed the pay book and sent it to Lewis' mother.

Memorials: Vis-en-Artois Memorial, France; Whitney Church, Whitney on Wye, Herefordshire; Brilley War Memorial, Herefordshire.

Location of VC: Believed still held by the family.

Citation for VC: L.G. 31st January, 1919.

"For most conspicuous bravery at Rossnoy, 18th September, 1918, when in command of a section on the right of an attacking line, held up by intense machine-gun fire. Lance-Corporal Lewis, observing that two enemy machine-guns were enfilading the line, crawled forward single-handed and successfully bombed the guns, and by rifle fire later caused the whole team to surrender thereby enabling the line to advance.

"On 21st September, 1918, he again displayed great powers of command and having rushed his company through the enemy barrage, was killed whilst getting his men under cover from heavy machine-gun fire. Throughout he showed a splendid disregard of danger, and his leadership at a critical period was beyond all praise."

The VC was presented to his parents by H.M. King George V at Buckingham Palace, 10th April, 1919.

C.S.M. JOHN WILLIAMS
10th South Wales Borderers

Full Name: John Henry Williams.

Place of Birth: Nantyglo, Monmouthshire.

Date of Birth: 29th September, 1886.

Father: Henry Williams.

Mother: Elizabeth Williams (schoolteacher).

Father's Occupation: —

Education: Brierley Hill Council School, Ebbw Vale, Monmouthshire.

Pre-Service Employment: Blacksmith at Cwm Colliery.

Service Record: Enlisted South Wales Borderers, 1906 (Service No. 20408); bought his discharge; enlisted 10th South Wales Borderers, 12th November, 1914; Sergeant, 1st January, 1915; served France and Flanders, 1915-18; Company Sergeant Major, 2nd October, 1917; severely wounded by shrapnel in right arm and leg, 1918; discharged unfit for active service,

17th October, 1918; served in Ebbw Vale Home Guard during the Second World War with the rank of Captain.

Rewards, Decorations and Medals: Victoria Cross (for action at Villers Outreaux, France, 7th/8th October, 1918); Distinguished Conduct Medal (for action at Mametz Wood, 10th/12th July, 1916); Military Medal (for action at Pilkem Ridge, 31st July, 1917, L.G. 28th September, 1917); Bar to Military Medal (for action at Armentieres, 30th October, 1917, where he brought in a wounded soldier, L.G. 23rd February, 1918); 1914-15 Star; British War Medal; Victory Medal (M. in D.); Coronation Medal (1937); Medaille Militaire (France, L.G. 15th December, 1919).

Post-Service Employment: Commissionaire, Steel, Iron & Coal Company, Ebbw Vale (until that company ceased trading during the 1930s); rent collector, Ebbw Vale Council; Commissionaire, Richard Baldwin & Thomas, Ebbw Vale from late 1930s until his death.

Married: 1) Gertrude Williams. They resided at 9 York Avenue, Garden City, Ebbw Vale. She died in 1928. 2) Morfydd Rees of Aberbeeg, Ebbw Vale, c. 1937.

Children: Five sons and five daughters.

Died: St. Woolos Hospital, Newport, Monmouthshire, 7th March, 1953. At the time his home was at 4 The Dingle, Queen's Square, Ebbw Vale.

Buried: Ebbw Vale Cemetery.

Memorials: The headstone, erected in Ebbw Vale Cemetery, was removed during cemetery clearance work; Council Offices, Ebbw Vale; General Office, Richard Baldwin and Thomas, Ebbw Vale.

Location of VC: South Wales Borderers Museum, Brecon.

Citation for VC: L.G. 14th December, 1918.
"For most conspicuous bravery, initiative and devotion to duty on the night of the 7th-8th October, 1918, during the attack on Villers Outreaux, when, observing that his company was suffering heavy casualties from an enemy machine gun, he ordered a Lewis gun to engage it, and went forward under heavy fire to the flank of the enemy post, which he rushed single-handed, capturing fifteen of the enemy. These prisoners, realising that Williams was alone turned on him and one of them gripped his rifle. He succeeded in breaking away and bayonetting five enemy, whereupon the remainder again surrendered. By this gallant action and total disregard of personal danger he was the means of enabling not only his own company but also those on the flanks to advance."

He was decorated with the VC by H.M. King George V at Buckingham Palace, 22nd February, 1919. At the same investiture he also received the DCM, MM and Bar to the MM, which is reputed to have been the first time that the King had decorated the same man four times in one day. At the time of the investiture Williams had not recovered from his severe wounds and during the presentation the wound in his arm opened up and had to be treated before he could leave the Palace. John Henry Williams is the most decorated Welsh Non-Commissioned Officer of all time.

Citation for DCM: L.G. 13th February, 1917.
"For conspicuous gallantry in action. He handled his men in the attack with great courage and skill. He has performed constant good work throughout."

93

LIEUTENANT WILLIAM BISSETT
1/6th Argyll and Sutherland Highlanders

Full Name: William Davidson Bissett.

Place of Birth: Bauchlands, St. Martins, Perthshire. The family later resided at Ewing Cottage, Comrie Road, Crieff, Perthshire.

Date of Birth: 7th August, 1893.

Father: John Bissett.

Mother: Nellie Milne Bissett (nee Davidson).

Father's Occupation: —

Education: Taylor's Institution, Crieff, Perthshire.

Pre-Service Employment: —

Service Record: Enlisted 6th Argyll and Sutherland Highlanders (Territorial Force), 29th April, 1912; mobilised, August, 1914; posted to France, 1st May, 1915; Lance Corporal, 25th July, 1915; Corporal, 24th October, 1915 (for services as a bomber in the trenches); Battery Bombing Sergeant, 1st May, 1916; commissioned 2nd Lieutenant, Argyll and Sutherland Highlanders, 19th December, 1916 (trained in England); returned to France, 12th May, 1917; rejoined his battalion, 22nd May, 1917; Lieutenant, 1918; wounded and gassed, 25th October, 1918 (during action east of Maing, France); returned to duty, 16th November, 1918; posted to Italy, 1918-19; hospitalised sick, 18th January, 1919; demobilised, 24th September, 1919; served Royal Army Ordnance Corps, rank of Captain, 15th May, 1939-23rd May, 1940; transferred to Royal Pioneer Corps, 24th May, 1940; demobilised, rank of Major, 22nd September, 1945.

Rewards, Decorations and Medals: Victoria Cross (for action east of Maing, France, 25th October, 1918); 1914-15 Star; British War Medal; Victory Medal; British War Medal (1939-45); Defence Medal; Coronation Medal (1937); Coronation Medal (1953); Croix de Guerre with Palms (France, 1918); Gold watch and War Bonds from the town of Crieff.

Post-Service Employment: He was involved in some form of private business in London and for a time resided at Walton-on-Thames. He later moved to Betws-Y-Coed, Caernarfonshire and later to Overton, Flintshire.

Married: Hilda Heywood, a nursing sister, at Emmanuel Parish Church, Hampstead, 1919.

Children: One son.

Died: 12th May, 1971, at Wrexham War Memorial Hospital, Denbighshire. He resided at the time at Queensbridge Hall, Overton-on-Dee, Flintshire. He was the last VC to live in North Wales.

Buried: Cremated at Wrexham Crematorium after a service at Overton-on-Dee Parish Church. His ashes were buried at Aldershot Military Cemetery.

Memorials: Aldershot Military Cemetery.

Location of VC: Argyll and Sutherland Highlanders Museum, Stirling Castle, Stirling.

Citation for VC: L.G. 6th January, 1919.
"For most conspicuous bravery and leadership East of Maing on the 25th October, 1918, when in command of a platoon, which he led to its objective with great dash. Later, owing to casualties, he took command of the company and handled it with great skill after a determined enemy counter-attack had turned his left flank. Realising the danger, he withdrew to the

railway, thus temporarily saving the situation. The enemy, however, continued to advance in force after his men had exhausted their ammunition. Thereupon, under heavy fire, he mounted the railway embankment and, calling upon his men to charge with the bayonet, drove back the enemy with heavy loss, and, later, again charging forward, established the line.

"By his splendid example and fine leadership Lieutenant Bissett was the means of saving a critical situation."

He was decorated with the VC by H.M. King George V at Buckingham Palace, 10th July, 1919.

ACTING LIEUTENANT COLONEL DUDLEY JOHNSON
South Wales Borderers, attached to 2nd Royal Sussex Regiment

Full Name: Dudley Graham Johnson.

Place of Birth: Rockcliffe, Bourton on the Water, Gloucestershire. The family later lived at Oddington, Moreton in Marsh, Gloucestershire.

Date of Birth: 13th February, 1884.

Father: Captain William Johnson.

Mother: Rosina Johnson, daughter of Sir John Arnott, proprietor of "The Irish Times".

Father's Occupation: Officer, Inniskilling Dragoons.

Education: Bradfield College.

Service Record: Enlisted 3rd Wiltshire Regiment of Militia, 1901; served on St. Helena, guarding Boer prisoners of war, 1901; commissioned 2nd Lieutenant, South Wales Borderers, 4th July, 1903; Lieutenant, 2nd March, 1907; Adjutant, 5th February, 1909-4th February, 1912; Captain, 11th March, 1914; served 2nd South Wales Borderers, Mauritius, Hong Kong, China, 1912-14; present at capture of Tsingtao, China, November, 1914; served Gallipoli, 1915 (wounded 25th April); GSO 3 Home Forces, 3rd December, 1915-24th May, 1916; Brigade Major, Home Forces, 25th May, 1916-22nd October, 1916; DAA & QMG, 1st Division, France, 5th January, 1917-27th December, 1917; Major, 4th December, 1917; Acting Lieutenant Colonel, 1st South Wales Borderers, 5th January, 1918-16th February, 1918; Acting Lieutenant Colonel, 2nd Royal Sussex Regiment, 5th April, 1918-31st December, 1918 (wounded, 27th May, 1918); Temporary Lieutenant Colonel (South Wales Borderers) commanding 2nd Royal Sussex Regiment, 1st January, 1919-24th April, 1919; served Germany, 1919; Chief Instructor (Class AA), Small Arms School, Hythe, 22nd September, 1919-21st September, 1923; Brevet Lieutenant Colonel, 29th September, 1923; Lieutenant Colonel, 29th December, 1923; attended Senior Officers' School, Belgaum, India, 1925; transferred 2nd North Staffordshire Regiment, 14th April, 1925; Chief Instructor (Class AA), Machine-gun School, Netheravon, 2nd December, 1926-11th April, 1928; Colonel, 29th December, 1927; GOC 12th (Secunderabad) Infantry Brigade (Temporary Brigadier), 1st July, 1933-20th January, 1936; Commandant Small Arms School, Netheravon and GOC Records, Small Arms School Corps (Temporary Brigadier), 13th February, 1936-6th January, 1938; Major General, 25th December, 1937; GOC 4th Division, 7th January, 1938-24th June, 1940; served France and Belgium, 1939-40 (present at the evacuation of the BEF from Dunkirk); GOC Aldershot Command, 25th June, 1940-12th March, 1941; Hon. Colonel, Monmouthshire Regiment, 1941; Inspector of Infantry, 21st March, 1941-30th April, 1942; retired 1944; Hon. Colonel, South Wales Borderers, 1944-49.

Rewards, Decorations and Medals: Victoria Cross (for action at Sambre Canal, France, 4th November, 1918); CB (1939); DSO (for action at the capture of Tsingtao, China, 5th/6th November, 1914); Bar to DSO (for action at Pontruet, 1918); Military Cross (L.G. January, 1918); Queen's South Africa Medal (no clasps); 1914-15 Star; British War Medal; Victory Medal (M. in D.); 1939-45 Star; Defence Medal; British War Medal (1939-45, M. in D.); Jubilee Medal (1935); Coronation Medal (1937); Coronation Medal (1953); ADC to H.M. King George VI (10th September, 1936-6th January, 1939).

Post-Service Employment: Retired General Officer; Borough Councillor, Fleet, Hampshire; President, Hampshire British Legion.

Married: Marjorie, daughter of Reverend Arthur George Grisewood, Rector of Daylesford, Chipping Norton, at Stow on the Wold, 12th June, 1912.

Children: One son, two daughters.

Died: 21st December, 1975, at 2 Heathfield Court, Fleet, Hampshire. He had previously resided at Orchard House, Church Crookham, Hampshire.

Buried: Church Crookham Cemetery, Hampshire.

Memorials: Church Crookham Church and Cemetery, Hampshire; Brecon Cathedral; General Johnson Homes (Royal British Legion), near Guildford, Surrey; Johnson Prize, Church Crookham School.

Location of VC: South Wales Borderers Museum, Brecon.

Citation for VC: L.G. 6th January, 1919.

"For most conspicuous bravery and leadership during the forcing of the Sambre Canal, France on the 4th November, 1918. The 2nd Infantry Brigade, of which the 2nd Battalion The Royal Sussex Regiment formed part, was ordered to cross by the lock south of Catillon. The position was strong and before the bridge could be taken a steep bank leading up to the lock and a waterway about 100 yards short of the canal had to be crossed. The assaulting platoons and bridging parties, Royal Engineers, on their arrival at the waterway were thrown into confusion by a heavy barrage and machine-gun fire and heavy casualties were caused. At this moment, Lt. Colonel Johnson arrived, and, realising the situation, at once collected men to man the bridges and assist the Royal Engineers and personally led the assault. In spite of his efforts heavy fire again broke up the assaulting and bridging parties. Without any hesitation, he again reorganised the platoons and bridging parties and led them at the lock, this time succeeding in effecting a crossing after which all went well. During all this time Lieutenant Colonel Johnson was under a very heavy fire, which, though it nearly decimated the assaulting columns, left him untouched. His conduct was a fine example of great valour, coolness and intrepidity which, added to his splendid leadership and the offensive spirit that he had inspired in his battalion, were entirely responsible for the successful crossing."

He was decorated with the VC by H.M. King George V at Buckingham Palace, 14th June, 1919. On the same occasion he also received the Bar to his DSO and the MC.

Citation for DSO: L.G. 16th March, 1915.

"For conspicuous ability on the night of 5th-6th November, 1914, during the operations against the German positions at Tsingtao, and for great gallantry in rescuing several wounded men whilst exposed to heavy fire."

Citation for Bar to DSO: L.G. 11th January, 1919.

"For conspicuous gallantry and devotion to duty in command of his battalion in the attack. The ground over which his battalion advanced was very difficult but thanks to his careful dispositions was successfully negotiated. He personally superintended after the objective was reached and subsequently carried out a night attack advancing some thousand yards in the face of strenuous opposition. His skilful arrangements and conduct throughout inspired the men under him with a splendid fighting spirit."

SERGEANT SAMUEL PEARSE
45th Royal Fusiliers

Full Name: Samuel George Pearse.

Place of Birth: Penarth, Glamorgan.

Date of Birth: 16th July, 1897.

Father: George Pearse.

Mother: —

Father's Occupation: Farmer.

Education: —

Pre-Service Employment: Emigrated with his family to Mildura, Victoria, Australia in 1911 where his father had a farm.

Service Record: Enlisted Australian Imperial Force, 2nd Company, 1st Machine Gun Battalion, 1915 (Service No. 2870); Lance Corporal, 21st November, 1917; Corporal, 10th April, 1918; discharged, 18th July, 1919; re-enlisted, 45th Royal Fusiliers for service in Northern Russia, rank Sergeant, July, 1919 (Service No. 133002).

Rewards, Decorations and Medals: Victoria Cross (for action north of Emtsa, Northern Russia, 29th August, 1919); Military Medal (for action at Ypres, 1917); 1914-15 Star; British War Medal; Victory Medal; Russian Order of St. George (?).

Married: Catherine, daughter of William West Knox of 3 Yard Row, Philadelphia, Newbottle, County Durham, 1st June, 1919.

Children: One daughter, born after his death.

Died: K. in A. near Emtsa, Northern Russia, 29th August, 1919.

Buried: Archangel Allied Cemetery, Russia.

Memorials: Archangel Allied Cemetery, Russia; Hall of Valour, Canberra, Australia.

Location of VC: Held by family.

Citation for VC: L.G. 23rd October, 1919.

"For most conspicuous bravery, devotion to duty and self sacrifice during operations against the enemy battery position north of Emtsa (north Russia) on 29th August, 1919. Sergeant Pearse cut his way through the enemy barbed wire under very heavy machine gun and rifle fire and cleared a way for the troops to enter the battery position. Seeing that a blockhouse was harrassing our advance and causing us casualties, he charged the blockhouse single handed, killing the occupants with bombs. This gallant non-commissioned officer met his death a minute later and it was due to him that the position was carried with so few casualties. His magnificent bravery and utter disregard for personal danger won for him the admiration of all troops."

The VC was presented to his widow by H.M. King George V at Buckingham Palace, 25th March, 1920.

CAPTAIN BERNARD WARBURTON-LEE, R.N.
HMS Hardy

Full Name: Bernard Armitage Warburton Warburton-Lee. The family surname was changed from Lee to Warburton-Lee by deed poll, 25th November, 1919.

Place of Birth: Broad Oak, Redbrook, Maelor, Flintshire.

Date of Birth: 13th September, 1895.

Father: Joseph Henry Warburton Warburton-Lee.

Mother: Eva Vernon Warburton-Lee (nee Armitage).

Father's Occupation: Barrister at Law, Landowner, High Sheriff of Flintshire.

Education: Malvern Link Preparatory School, Worcesterhire, 1906; Osborne College, Isle of Wight, 1908-10; Dartmouth College (passed top of his term) 1910-12.

Service Record: Passed out from the training cruiser HMS Cornwall, 1912; Midshipman, HMS Hyacinth (Light Cruiser), 15th January, 1913-August, 1915, stationed at Cape Town; present during the search for and sinking of the German Light Cruiser Koenigsberg, East Africa, 1915; Sub-Lieutenant, 15th July, 1915; Sub-Lieutenant, HMS Cherwell (Torpedo Boat Destroyer), 15th September, 1915-4th January, 1916; served Grand Fleet; Sub-Lieutenant, HMS Mameluke (M-Class Destroyer), 4th January, 1916-15th April, 1917; Acting Lieutenant, HMS Mischief (M-Class Destroyer), 24th April, 1917-16th April, 1918; Lieutenant, 15th January, 1918; Lieutenant, HMS Wrestler (W-Class Destroyer), 16th April, 1918-12th April, 1921; attended Royal Naval College, Greenwich (Gunnery Theoretical Course), 21st April, 1921-March, 1922; served HMS Marlborough, 13th August, 1922-1924; Royal Naval College, Greenwich (Signals and Wireless Transmission Course), 1924; O.C. HMS Tuscan (Destroyer, 8th Flotilla, Atlantic Fleet), 28th November, 1924-15th January, 1925; Lieutenant Commander, 15th January, 1925; O.C. HMS Sterling (Destroyer, 8th Flotilla, Atlantic Fleet), 15th January, 1925; O.C. HMS Walpole (Destroyer, 6th Flotilla, Atlantic Fleet), 30th March, 1926; commanded a RN detachment which guarded the Vickers Yard at Barrow during the General Strike, May, 1926; O.C. HMS Vanessa (Destroyer, 2nd Flotilla, Mediterranean Fleet), 9th April, 1929-3rd June, 1930; Commander, 30th June, 1930; Staff Course, Royal Naval College, Greenwich, 13th January, 1931; Staff College, Camberley, 21st May, 1932; O.C. HMS Centurion, 21st January, 1933-6th April, 1933; O.C. HMS Bryony (Despatch Vessel, Mediterranean Fleet), 23rd April, 1933; O.C. HMS Witch (Destroyer), October, 1934-13th August, 1936; Captain, 30th June, 1936; Imperial Defence College, 12th January, 1937; Tactical Course, Portsmouth, 10th January, 1938; Flag Captain, O.C. HMS Hawkins (Light Cruiser) and Chief of Staff to the Vice Admiral Commanding the Reserve Fleet at Portsmouth, 14th February, 1938; Flag Captain, O.C. HMS Effingham (Cruiser), and Chief of Staff to Vice Admiral Commanding the Reserve Fleet, Portsmouth, 21st June, 1938; Tactical Course, Portsmouth, 8th May, 1939; O.C. 2nd Destroyer Flotilla, HMS Hardy, Mediterranean Fleet, 28th July, 1939; O.C. 2nd Destroyer Flotilla, HMS Hardy, Norway, as part of the Naval force sent to that country following the German invasion in April, 1940; present at the first Battle of Narvik, 10th April, 1940.

Rewards, Decorations and Medals: Victoria Cross (for action at Narvik, Norway, 10th April, 1940); 1914 Star; British War Medal; Victory Medal (M. in D. for services in the Grand Fleet Destroyers between 1st January and 30th June, 1918); 1939-45 Star; Atlantic Star; British War Medal (1939-45, M. in D.); Norwegian War Cross (L.G. 13th October, 1942, for distinguished services in the Allied cause during the Campaign in Norway); Jubilee Medal (1935); Coronation Medal (1937).

Married: Elizabeth, daughter of Captain Campbell-Swinton at St. James' Church, Sussex Gardens, London, 1924.

Children: One son.

Died: Died of wounds, Narvik, Norway, 10th April, 1940.

Buried: Ballangen New Cemetery, Narvik, Norway, British Plot 4, Row B, Grave 9.

Memorials: Ballangen New Cemetery, Narvik, Norway; Whitewell Church, Maelor, Flintshire; Iscoed War Memorial, Maelor, Flintshire; Warburton-Lee Lodge of the Sons of England Patriotic and Benevolent Society, Klerlsdorp, South Africa.

Location of VC: Held by the family.

Citation for VC: L.G. 7th June, 1940.

"For gallantry, enterprise and daring in command of the Force engaged in the first Battle of Narvik, on the 10th April, 1940. On being ordered to carry out an attack on Narvik, he learned from Tranoy that the enemy held the place in much greater force than had been thought. He signalled to the Admiralty that the enemy were reported to be holding Narvik in force, that six destroyers and one submarine were there, that the channel might be mined, and that he intended to attack at dawn, high water. The Admiralty replied that two Norwegian Coast Defence Ships might be in German hands, that he alone could judge whether to attack, and that whatever decision he made would have full support. Captain Warburton-Lee gave out the plan for his attack and led his Flotilla of five Destroyers up the Fjord in heavy snowstorms, arriving off Narvik just after daybreak. He took the enemy completely by surprise and made three successful attacks on warships and merchantmen in the harbour. The last attack was made after anxious debate. On the Flotilla withdrawing, five enemy Destroyers of superior gun-power were encountered and engaged. The Captain was mortally wounded by a shell which hit 'Hardy's' bridge. His last signal was 'Continue to engage the enemy'."

The VC was presented to his widow and son by H.M. King George VI at Buckingham Palace, 2nd July, 1940. It was the first VC to be gazetted in the Second World War.

LIEUTENANT THE HONOURABLE CHRISTOPHER FURNESS
1st Welsh Guards

Full Name: The Honourable Christopher Furness.

Place of Birth: 5 Cambridge Gate, London, N.W.1.

Date of Birth: 17th May, 1912.

Father: Marmaduke Furness, 1st Viscount Furness (1918), 2nd Baron Furness (1910).

Mother: Daisy Furness, Viscountess Furness.

Father's Occupation: Ship owner and builder, racehorse breeder, active in coal and iron industries.

Education: Eton College, 1925-29 (served as a Private in the OTC).

Pre-Service Employment: Details not known.

Service Record: Served Welsh Guards Reserve of Officers, 27th July, 1932-1st September, 1939 (Service No. 53422); Lieutenant, 24th August, 1939; called up for active service, 2nd September, 1939; embarked for service in France and Belgium with 1st Welsh Guards, 26th November, 1939.

Rewards, Decorations and Medals: Victoria Cross (for action near Arras, France, 24th May, 1940); 1939-45 Star; British War Medal (1939-45).

Married: Not married. He was, at the time of his death, engaged to be married to Princess Natasha Bagration (cousin to Princess Marina, Duchess of Kent).

Children: None.

Died: St. Laurent, near Arras, France, 24th May, 1940. He was posted missing presumed killed until 1946.

Buried: No known grave.

Memorials: Dunkirk Memorial, France, Column 34. Eton College, Chapel; Guards Chapel Roll of Honour, Wellington Barracks, London.

Location of VC: RHQ, The Welsh Guards.

Citation for VC: L.G. 7th February, 1946.

"Lieutenant Furness was in command of the Carrier Platoon, Welsh Guards, during the period 17th/24th May, 1940, when his battalion formed part of the garrison of Arras. During this time his platoon was constantly patrolling in advance of or between the widely dispersed parts of the perimeter and fought many local actions with the enemy. Lieutenant Furness displayed the highest qualities of leadership and dash on all these occasions and imbued his command with a magnificent offensive spirit. During the evening of 23rd May, Lieutenant Furness was wounded when on patrol but he refused to be evacuated. By this time the enemy, considerably reinforced, had encircled the town on three sides and withdrawal to Douai was ordered during the night of 23rd-24th May. Lieutenant Furness's platoon, together with a small force of light tanks, were ordered to cover the withdrawal of the transport, consisting of over 40 vehicles. About 0.230 hours on 24th May the enemy attacked on both sides of the town. At one point the enemy advanced to the road along which the transport columns were withdrawing, bringing them under very heavy small arms and anti-tank gun fire. Thus the whole column was blocked and placed in serious jeopardy. Immediately, Lieutenant Furness, appreciating the seriousness of the situation and in spite of his wounds, decided to attack the enemy, who were located in a strongly entrenched position behind the wire. Lieutenant Furness advanced with three Carriers supported by light tanks. At once the enemy opened up with very heavy fire from small arms and anti-tank guns. The light tanks were put out of action but Lieutenant Furness continued to advance. He reached the enemy position and circled it several times at close range, inflicting heavy losses. All 3 Carriers were hit and most of their crews killed or wounded. His own Carrier was disabled and the driver and Bren-gunner killed. He then engaged the enemy in personal hand-to-hand combat until he was killed. His magnificent act of self-sacrifice against hopeless odds and when already wounded, made the enemy withdraw for the time being and enabled the large column of vehicles to get clear unmolested and covered the evacuation of some of the wounded of his own Carrier Platoon and the light tanks."

The VC was presented to his half-brother, 2nd Viscount Furness, by H.M. King George VI at Buckingham Palace, 30th July, 1946.

SQUADRON LEADER HUGHIE EDWARDS
105 Squadron, R.A.F.

Full Name: Hughie Idwal Edwards.

Place of Birth: Masman Park, Perth, Western Australia.

Date of Birth: 1st August, 1914.

Father: Hugh Edwards (formerly of Pant-Y-Fa Farm, Llwyn Gwril, Merioneth and Felin Newydd, Llandrillo, Nr. Corwen, Merionethshire. He emigrated to Australia c. 1909).

Mother: Jane Edwards (nee Watkins, formerly of Llanfaircaerenion, Montgomeryshire).

Father's Occupation: Blacksmith, Fremantle Gold Mine. Later Engineer, Perth Public Works Department.

Education: White Gam Valley School; Fremantle Boys' School, Perth.

Pre-Service Employment: Clerk in a shipping office in Fremantle.

Service Record: Enlisted Royal Australian Garrison Artillery, Fremantle, 1934, as a Private; enlisted Royal Australian Air Force, 1935; qualified as a pilot, June, 1936; transferred to the Royal Air Force as a Pilot Officer, 21st August, 1936 (Service No. 39005); posted to No. 15 Squadron at Abingdon, later moving to Tern Hill (flying Hawker Hinds); posted to No. 90 Squadron, March, 1937 (flying Bristol Blenheims); appointed Adjutant; Flying Officer, 21st May, 1938; seriously injured his right leg whilst baling out of an aircraft, August, 1938, and hospitalised for nine months, returned to flying duties in April, 1940; posted to No. 139 Squadron, February, 1941 (flying Bristol Blenheims); O.C. 105 Squadron, 11th May, 1941 (flying Bristol Blenheims); posted to Malta, 28th July, 1941; Squadron Leader, 8th August, 1941; sent on a lecture tour of the United States, October, 1941; Chief Flying Instructor, Wellesbourne Mountford; O.C. 105 Squadron, 3rd August, 1942 (flying De Havilland Mosquitos); Temporary Wing Commander, 1st September, 1942; Temporary Group Captain, 2nd February, 1943; O.C. RAF Binbrook; posted Ceylon, Group Captain, Bombing Operations, RAF HQ Kandy, December, 1944; Station Administrative Officer, HQ South East Asia Command, January, 1945; Wing Commander, 1st July, 1947; graduated Staff Course, Bracknell, 1949; SPSO 21 Group HQ Flying Training Command, 1949-50; O.C. Flying Wing, RAF Brize Norton, 1950-51; O.C. Flying Wings, RAF Wyton and Benson, 1951-53; O.C. RAF Wattisham, 1953-56; Group Captain, 1st January, 1954; O.C. RAF Habbanuja, Iraq, 1956-58; Acting Air Commodore, 23rd October, 1958; Commandant Central Flying Establishment, RAF West Raynham, 1958-60; Air Commodore, 1st July, 1959; Imperial Defence College, 1961; Director of Establishments (RAF), Air Ministry, 1962-63; retired 30th September, 1963.

Rewards, Decorations and Medals: Victoria Cross (for action over Bremen, 4th July, 1941); KCMG (L.G. 1974); CB (L.G. 1st January, 1959); DSO (for action during a raid on the Phillips Factory, Eindhoven, Holland,

6th December, 1942); OBE (L.G. 11th February, 1947); DFC (L.G. 1st July, 1941); 1939-45 Star; Air Crew Europe Star; Burma Star; British War Medal (1939-45); Defence Medal; Coronation Medal (1953); ADC to H.M. Queen Elizabeth II, 1960-63 (L.G. March, 1960).

Post-Service Employment: Australian Resident Director, Selection Trust, 1964-74; Governor of Western Australia, 1974 (retired due to ill health, 2nd April, 1975).

Married: 1) Linda Cherry, widow of Flt. Lt. H. R. A. Beresford, 21st January, 1942 (she died in 1966). She was the daughter of Group Captain A. E. Barr-Simm, of London. 2) Mrs. Dorothy Carrew Berrick, 1972.

Children: One son and one daughter.

Died: 5th August, 1982, Sydney, New South Wales, Australia.

Buried: Cremated.

Memorials: Australian War Memorial, Canberra; Fremantle Boys' School, Australia.

Location of VC: Hall of Valour, Canberra, Australia.

Citation for VC: L.G. 22nd July, 1941.

"Wing Commander Edwards, although handicapped by a physical disability arising from a flying accident, has repeatedly displayed gallantry of the highest order in pressing home bombing attacks from very low heights against strongly defended objectives.

"On 4th July, 1941, he led an important attack on the Port of Bremen, one of the most heavily defended towns in Germany. This attack had to be made in daylight and there were no clouds to afford concealment. During the approach to the German coast several enemy ships were sighted and Wing Commander Edwards knew that his aircraft would be reported and that the defences would be in a state of readiness. Undaunted by this misfortune, he brought his formation for miles overland to the target, flying at a height of little more than 50 feet, passing under high tension cables, carrying away telegraph wires and finally passing through a formidable balloon barrage. On reaching Bremen he was met with a hail of fire, all his aircraft being hit and four of them being destroyed. Nevertheless, he made a most successful attack, and then with the greatest skill and coolness withdrew the surviving aircraft without further loss.

"Throughout the execution of this operation which he had planned personally with full knowledge of the risks entailed, Wing Commander Edwards displayed the highest possible standard of gallantry and determination."

He was decorated with the VC by H.M. King George VI at Buckingham Palace, 17th February, 1942. He received his DFC at the same investiture.

Citation for DFC: L.G. 1st July, 1941.

"In June, 1941, this officer led a formation of aircraft on an operational sweep against enemy shipping off the Dutch coast. A convoy of eight merchant vessels was sighted at anchor about 3 miles outside The Hague. In the face of intense and accurate pompom and machine gun fire, the formation attacked from a height of only 50 feet. Wing Commander Edwards attacked a ship of some 4,000 tons and, after raking the decks with his forward machine guns, released his bombs from mast high. A considerable explosion followed, debris being thrown in the air while columns of black smoke were emitted. The vessel was certainly severely damaged if not sunk. This officer has completed operational missions over enemy and enemy occupied country, and against their shipping and has at all times displayed great leadership, skill and gallantry."

LIEUTENANT COMMANDER STEPHEN BEATTIE, R.N.
HMS Campbeltown

Full Name: Stephen Halden Beattie.

Place of Birth: The Vicarage, Leighton, Montgomeryshire. The family later resided at Ross-on-Wye.

Date of Birth: 29th March, 1908.

Father: Rev. Prebendary Ernest Halden Beattie, MC (originally of Perth, Scotland).

Mother: Ethel Beattie (nee Knowles).

Father's Occupation: Vicar of Treslystan with Leighton.

Education: Abberley Hall; Rugby School, January, 1922-1925 (School House).

Service Record: Joined the Royal Navy by Special Entry directly from school, September, 1925; Special Entry Cadet, 15th November, 1925; served on Training Ships HMS Thunderer and HMS Erebus; Midshipman, HMS Barham, 1st January, 1927; Lieutenant, 15th November, 1930; Lieutenant Commander, 1st November, 1938; serving HMS Zulu, 1939; O.C. HMS Vivien (V Class Destroyer), 1940; shot down two enemy aircraft in the North Sea, November, 1940 and, the same month, Mentioned in Despatches for action against E-Boats; ordered to stand-by in command of HMS Petard (under construction), January, 1942; O.C. HMS Campbeltown (ex-US Navy, 4 funnel destroyer), March, 1942; St. Nazaire Raid, France, 27th March, 1942; P.O.W. Marlag und Milag Nord, Bremen, 1942-45 (M. in D. for his conduct whilst a Prisoner of War); Commander, 30th June, 1945; served HMS Whirlwind and HMS Zodiac; Captain, 30th June, 1951; Senior Officer, 1st Australian Frigate Squadron, 1952-54; Senior Naval Officer, Persian Gulf, 1956-58; O.C. HMS Birmingham 1958; retired 1960.

Rewards, Decorations and Medals: Victoria Cross (for action at St. Nazaire, France, whilst commanding HMS Campbeltown, 27th March, 1942); 1939-45 Star; Atlantic Star; France and Germany Star; British War Medal (M. in D.); Croix de Guerre with Palms (France, 1947); Legion of Honour (1947).

Post-Service Employment: O.C. Nautical College, Accra, Ghana, 1960-65; Naval Advisor to the Ethiopian Government, Spring, 1965-November, 1969.

Married: Philippa Mary, daughter of Paymaster Rear-Admiral Edward Charles Blanchflower, 1933.

Children: Four sons.

Died: 24th April, 1975, at his home Salt House, Mullion, Cornwall.

Buried: Ruan Minor Churchyard, Cornwall, 28th April, 1975.

Memorials: Ruan Minor Churchyard, Cornwall.

Location of VC: Held by his family.

Citation for VC: L.G. 21st May, 1942.

"For great gallantry and determination in the attack on St. Nazaire (March 27th, 1942) in command of HMS Campbeltown. Under intense fire directed at the bridge from point blank range of about 100 yards, and in the full blinding glare of many searchlights, he steamed her into the lock gates and beached and scuttled her in the correct position.

"This VC was awarded in recognition, not only of his own valour but also of the unnamed officers and men of a very gallant ship's company, many of whom have not returned."

He was decorated with the VC by H.M. King George VI at Buckingham Palace, 22nd June, 1945.

N.B. Beattie was informed that he had been awarded the Victoria Cross at a full parade called by the commandant of his P.O.W. camp in Germany.

COMMANDER JOHN LINTON, R.N.
HM Submarine Turbulent

Full Name: John Wallace Linton.

Place of Birth: Claremont, Malpas, Newport, Monmouthshire.

Date of Birth: 15th October, 1905.

Father: Edward Maples Barron Linton.

Mother: Margaret Gertrude Linton (nee Wallace).

Father's Occupation: Architect.

Education: Osborne College, 1919; Dartmouth College, 1921-22 (2nd Prize for Mathematics).

Service Record: Midshipman, HMS Dauntless, 15th September, 1923; HMS Royal Oak, 1st January, 1925; Acting Sub-Lieutenant, 15th January, 1926; Lieutenant's Course, RN College, Greenwich, 1926; Lieutenant's Course, Portsmouth, 1927; Sub-Lieutenant, 15th July, 1927; HM Submarine L.22, 5th Submarine Flotilla, Portsmouth, 21st November, 1927; HM Submarine Oberon, 5th Submarine Flotilla, Portsmouth, 15th April, 1928; Lieutenant, 1st July, 1928; HM Submarine H.43, 5th Submarine Flotilla, Portsmouth, 12th August, 1929; HM Submarine Oswald, 3rd Submarine Flotilla, China, 16th January, 1932; Submarine Commander's Course, 1934-5; Lieutenant commanding HM Submarine L.21, 5th Submarine Flotilla, 3rd May, 1935; HM Submarine Snapper, 15th August, 1935; Lieutenant Commander, 1st July, 1936; HMS Iron Duke, Portsmouth, 11th May, 1936; HMS Medway, 4th Submarine Flotilla, China, 25th April, 1938; HM Submarine Pandora, 4th Submarine Flotilla, China, October, 1938; recalled to Alexandria, 1940; served 8th Submarine Flotilla, Gibraltar, December, 1940; HM Submarine Turbulent, 18th November, 1941; Commander, 31st December, 1941; sailed in command of Turbulent, 3rd January, 1942, arriving Alexandria, February, 1942; sank over 100,000 tons of enemy shipping (including 1 Cruiser, 1 Destroyer, 1 U-Boat, 28 supply ships and even destroyed three railway trains by ship to shore gunfire); sailed on his last patrol, 1st March, 1943; last sighted off Corsica, 14th March, 1943; believed that HM Submarine Turbulent hit a mine at the entrance to Maddalena Harbour, Italy, 23rd March, 1943, and sank with all hands.

Rewards, Decorations and Medals: Victoria Cross (for continual service in submarines from the outbreak of war until his last patrol in March, 1943); DSO (for service in submarines, L.G. September, 1942); DSC; 1939-45 Star; Africa Star; British War Medal, 1939-45.

Married: Nancy Kate Pitts-Tucker at Lutterworth, 1929.

Children: Two sons (the eldest died 17th April, 1951, when HM Submarine

Affray failed to surface in the English Channel).

Died: He is believed to have died, with his crew, when his submarine was sunk by enemy vessels off the coast of Corsica, 1943.

Buried: His body was never recovered.

Memorials: Portsmouth Naval Memorial, Panel 72, Column 3.

Location of VC: Held by his family.

Citation for VC: L.G. 25th May, 1943.

"From the outbreak of war until HMS Turbulent's last patrol, Commander Linton was constantly in command of submarines, and during that time inflicted great damage on the Enemy. He sank one Cruiser, one Destroyer, one U-boat, twenty-eight Supply Ships, some 100,000 tons in all, and destroyed three trains by gun-fire. In his last year he spent two hundred and fifty-four days at sea, submerged for nearly half the time, and his ship was hunted thirteen times and had two hundred and fifty depth charges aimed at her.

"His many and brilliant successes were due to his constant activity and skill, and the daring which never failed him when there was an Enemy to be attacked.

"On one occasion, for instance, in HMS Turbulent, he sighted a convoy of two Merchantmen and two Destroyers in mist and moonlight. He worked round ahead of the convoy and dived to attack it as it passed through the moon's rays. On bringing his sights to bear he found himself right ahead of a Destroyer. Yet he held his course till the Destroyer was almost on top of him, and, when his sights came on the convoy, he fired. His great courage and determination were rewarded. He sank one Merchantman and one Destroyer outright and set the other Merchantman on fire so that she blew up."

Linton's award was not posthumous as at the time of the announcement he was officially recorded as missing. The VC and DSO were presented to his widow and eldest son by H.M. King George VI at Buckingham Palace, 23rd February, 1944.

N.B. John Linton was a keen sportsman and had been capped several times for the R.N. Rugby Team between 1927 and 1930. He played in a trial match for England in 1927 and for Hampshire and the United Services during the same period.

The total tonnage sunk by Linton during the Second World War is the second highest of any British submarine commander. In 1942 he achieved the unique record of firing one salvo of three torpedos and sinking three enemy ships.

LIEUTENANT TASKER WATKINS
1/5th Welch Regiment

Full Name: Tasker Watkins.

Place of Birth: 19 Shingrig Road, Nelson, Glamorgan.

Date of Birth: 18th November, 1918.

Father: Betram Watkins.

Mother: Jane Watkins.

Father's Occupation: —

Education: Pontypridd Grammar School.

Pre-Service Employment: —

Service Record: Served in the ranks 16th October, 1939-16th May, 1941; granted Emergency Commission as 2nd Lieutenant, The Welch Regiment, 17th May, 1941 (Service No. P187088); joined 19th Welch Regiment, 24th May, 1941; War Substantive Lieutenant, 3rd April, 1942; joined 18th Welch Regiment, 30th November, 1942; Advanced Handling and Fieldcraft School, Llanberis, Caernarfonshire, 9th September, 1943; Instructor, Rifle Wing, Advanced Handling and Fieldcraft School, Llanberis, Caernarfonshire, 1st October, 1943; Acting Captain, 1st October, 1943; posted to 103 Reinforcement Group, British Liberation Army, 27th June, 1944; served Normandy and Northern Europe; joined 1/5th Welch Regiment, 25th July, 1944; relinquished rank of Temporary Captain, 25th July, 1944; Temporary Captain, 12th August, 1944; Acting Major, 22nd September, 1944; wounded in action, 27th October, 1944; returned to UK, 2nd November, 1944; Temporary Major and War Substantive Captain, 22nd December, 1944; posted 140 Officer Cadet Training Unit as Instructor, 26th January, 1945; posted to 164 Officer Cadet Training Unit as Instructor, 6th December, 1945; released from Military Service, 28th May, 1946; relinquished his Commission, 1st July, 1959.

Rewards, Decorations and Medals: Victoria Cross (for action at Barfour, Normandy, 16th August, 1944); 1939-45 Star; France and Germany Star; Defence Medal; British War Medal (1939-45); Knighthood, 1971; Deputy Lieutenant of the County of Glamorgan, 1956.

Married: Eirwen Evans, 1941.

Children: One son and one daughter.

Post-Service Employment: Called to the Bar, Middle Temple, 1948; Queen's Counsel, 1965; Chairman, Mental Health Review Tribunal (Wales Region), 1960-71; Deputy Chairman, Radnor Quarter Sessions, 1962-71; Deputy Chairman, Carmarthenshire Quarter Sessions, 1962-71; Bencher, 1970; Recorder, Merthyr Tydfil, 1968-70; Recorder, Swansea, 1970-71; Leader, Wales and Chester Circuit, 1970-71; Counsel (Deputy Attorney General) to Aberfan Inquiry, 1966; Judge, High Court of Justice (Queen's Bench Division), 1974; Judge, High Court of Justice (Family Division), 1971-74; Presiding Judge, Wales and Chester Circuit, 1975; President, Royal British Legion (Wales); Lord Justice of Appeal, 15th April, 1980; first Senior Presiding Judge for England and Wales, 27th July, 1983.

Location of VC: Held by Sir Tasker Watkins.

Citation for VC: L.G. 2nd November, 1944.

"On the evening of 16th August, 1944, a Battalion of The Welch Regiment attacked objectives near Barfour. Lieutenant Watkins' company came under murderous machine gun fire while advancing through corn fields set with booby traps. At the head of his men, Lieutenant Watkins, now the only officer left, charged two machine gun posts, personally accounting for the occupants with his Sten gun. Later, his gun jamming, he threw it in the face of a German anti-tank gunner, killing him at the same moment with a pistol shot. His small remnant counter attacked. Lieutenant Watkins led a bayonet charge, destroying the enemy, and finally at dusk, their wireless gone and separated from the Battalion which had withdrawn, he ordered his men to scatter, and himself personally charging and silencing an enemy machine gun post, he brought them back safely. This Officer's superb leadership not only saved his men's lives but decisively influenced the course of the battle."

He was decorated with the VC by H.M. King George VI at Buckingham Palace, 8th March, 1945.

FLIGHT LIEUTENANT DAVID LORD
271 Squadron, RAF

Full Name: David Samuel Anthony Lord.

Place of Birth: St. Mary's Avenue, Cork, Ireland (the family home whilst his father was stationed in Cork with the Royal Welch Fusiliers). They later lived at 15 Cilcern Grove, Wrexham, Denbighshire, and also at 22 Sandringham Road, Wrexham, Denbighshire.

Date of Birth: 18th October, 1913.

Father: Samuel Beswick Lord, MSM.

Mother: Mary Ellen Lord (nee Miller) of Cork, Ireland.

Father's Occupation: Warrant Officer, Royal Welch Fusiliers. He was later employed as a civilian clerical officer at the RWF Depot, Hightown Barracks, Wrexham, Denbighshire.

Education: Lucknow Convent School, Lucknow, India; St. Mary's RC School, Wrexham; St. Mary's College, Aberystwyth, Cardiganshire; English Ecclesiastical College, Valladolid, Spain.

Pre-Service Employment: On leaving school he began to train as a Roman Catholic priest but gave it up and returned to his home in Wrexham in 1934 where he was employed as a Photographer's Assistant by Francis & Co., Hope Street, Wrexham, until 1936. Freelance journalist, London, 1936.

Service Record: Enlisted Royal Air Force, 6th August, 1936 (six years service) as AC2/ACH (Service No. 49149); commenced pilot training at No. 3 Elementary and Reserve Flying Training School, Hamble, 6th October, 1938; first solo flight, 20th October, 1938; No. 2, Flying Training School, RAF Brize Norton, January, 1939; Sergeant Pilot, 5th April, 1939; Advanced Training Course, Warmwell; posted to 31 Squadron, Lahore, India (Vickers Valentia bombers); Supply Pilot, N.W. Frontier; conversion training to Douglas DC-2, June, 1941; transferred to Egypt for operations against the Italians in the Western Desert, October, 1941 (crashed, wounded slightly); Warrant Officer; returned to India, February, 1942; Captain, Douglas DC-3, April, 1942; Captain, C-53 Skytrooper, 14th June, 1942; Commissioned Pilot Officer, 12th July, 1942; supply operations to Burma, 1942/3 (Mentioned in Despatches); returned to Britain, 6th January, 1944; joined 271 Squadron, Doncaster, 29th January, 1944; training to drop men and supplies by parachute at Doncaster and as a glider tug at Down Ampney; dropped paratroops into Normandy on D-Day, 6th June, 1944; supply missions to Normandy and Northern France, 1944; dropped paratroops over Arnhem, 17th September, 1944; glider tug carrying reinforcements to Arnhem, 18th September, 1944; parachute re-supply mission to Arnhem, 19th September, 1944.

Rewards, Decorations and Medals: Victoria Cross (for action over Arnhem, Holland, 19th September, 1944); DFC (L.G. 16th July, 1943); 1939-45 Star; Air Crew Europe Star; Africa Star; Burma Star; France and Germany Star; British War Medal (M. in D.); India General Service Medal, 1936-39 (clasp North West Frontier, 1937-39).

Married: Not married.

Children: None.

Died: K. in A., 19th September, 1944, Arnhem, Holland.

Buried: Plot 4, Row B, Grave 5, Oosterbeek Military Cemetery, Arnhem, Holland.

Memorials: Oosterbeek Military Cemetery, Arnhem, Holland; Memorial Hall, Wrexham; St. Mary's RC Pro-Cathedral, Wrexham; St. Mary's RC School, Wrexham; Catholic Club, Wrexham; The Lord Trophy (presented to RAF Transport Command by his family and awarded annually to the medium range squadron gaining the highest score in a parachute and supply dropping contest); VC-10 (No. XR810) named 'David Lord, VC', November, 1968; Down Ampney Church, Gloucestershire.

Location of VC: Held by the family.

Citation for VC: L.G. 13th November, 1945.

"Flight Lieutenant Lord was the pilot and captain of a Dakota Aircraft detailed to drop supplies at Arnhem on the afternoon of September 19th, 1944. Our airborne troops had been surrounded and were being pressed into a small area defended by a large number of anti-aircraft guns. All crews were warned that intense opposition would be met over the dropping zone. To ensure accuracy they were ordered to fly at 900 feet when dropping their containers.

"While flying at 1,500 feet over Arnhem, the starboard wing of Flight Lieutenant Lord's aircraft was twice hit by anti-aircraft fire. The starboard engine was set on fire. He would have been justified in leaving the main stream of supplying aircraft and continuing at the same height or even abandoning his aircraft. But, on learning that his crew were uninjured and that the dropping zone would be reached in three minutes, he said he would complete his mission, as the troops were in dire need of supplies.

"By now the starboard engine was burning furiously. Flight Lieutenant Lord came down to 900 feet where he was singled out for the concentrated fire of the anti-aircraft guns. On reaching the dropping zone he kept the aircraft on a straight and level course while the supplies were dropped. At the end of the run he was told that two containers remained. Although he must have known that the collapse of the starboard wing could not be long delayed, Flight Lieutenant Lord circled, rejoined the stream of aircraft and made a second run to drop the remaining supplies. These manoeuvres took eight minutes in all, the aircraft being continuously under heavy anti-aircraft fire.

"His task completed, Flight Lieutenant Lord ordered the crew to abandon the Dakota, making no attempt himself to leave the aircraft which was down to 500 feet. A few seconds later the starboard wing collapsed and the aircraft fell in flames. There was only one survivor who was flung out whilst assisting other members of the crew to put on their parachutes.

"By continuing his mission in a damaged and burning aircraft, descending to drop the supplies accurately, returning to the dropping zone a second time and, finally, remaining at the controls to give his crew a chance to escape, Flight Lieutenant Lord displayed supreme valour and self-sacrifice."

The VC was presented to his parents by H.M. King George VI at Buckingham Palace on 18th December, 1945.

N.B. The delay in the announcement of the VC to David Lord was caused by the fact that the full story of his gallant action did not come out until the one surviving crewman, Flight Lieutenant Harry King, was released from a P.O.W. camp in 1945. Lord's VC was the only one awarded to RAF Transport Command.

CORPORAL EDWARD CHAPMAN
3rd Monmouthshire Regiment

Full Name: Edward Thomas Chapman.

Place of Birth: Pen Y Graig, Pontlottyn, Glamorgan.

Date of Birth: 13th January, 1920.

Father: Evan John Chapman.

Mother: Rachel Chapman (nee Saunders of Tirphil, Tredegar).

Father's Occupation: Collier.

Education: Fochrhiw School, Fochrhiw (until the age of 14 years).

Pre-Service Employment: Collier, Ogilvy Colliery, Deri.

Service Record: Enlisted in the Monmouthshire Regiment, 19th April, 1940 (Service No. 4080657); served North West Europe, 25th June, 1944-22nd May, 1946 (present at the fighting for Normandy and Northern France, the Low Countries, Rhine Crossing and North West Germany); wounded in the leg, 2nd April, 1945; released to Royal Army Reserve, 21st August, 1946; discharged from the Reserve on re-enlistment into the Territorial Army (Monmouthshire Regiment), 20th October, 1948 (Service No. 22243251); discharged on termination of engagement, 19th October, 1953; re-enlisted in the Territorial Army (Monmouthshire Regiment), 25th January, 1954; discharged on termination of engagement, 24th January, 1957, with the rank of Company Sergeant Major.

Rewards, Decorations and Medals: Victoria Cross (for action in the Teutoberger Wald, Germany, 2nd April, 1945); BEM (for services in the Territorial Army); 1939-45 Star; France and Germany Star; Defence Medal; British War Medal; Coronation Medal (1953); Jubilee Medal (1977).

Post-Service Employment: Rhymny Engineering; Great Western Railway, Station Porter at Pontlottyn, Glamorgan; ICI Fibres, Pontypool, Nylon Spinner (25 years service) until his retirement in 1980.

Married: Rhoda Frances Jean Watkins of Belfast, Northern Ireland, 1942.

Children: Three.

Location of VC: Held by Edward Chapman.

Citation for VC: L.G. 13th July, 1945.

"On 2nd April, 1945, a Company of the Monmouthshire Regiment crossed the Dortmund-Ems canal and was ordered to assault the ridge of the Teutoberger Wald, which dominates the surrounding country. This ridge is steep, thickly wooded and is ideal defensive country. It was, moreover, defended by a battalion of German officer cadets and their instructors, all of them picked men and fanatical Nazis.

"Corporal Chapman was advancing with his section in single file along a narrow track, when the enemy suddenly opened fire with machine-guns at short range, inflicting heavy casualties and causing some confusion. Corporal Chapman immediately ordered his section to take cover and, seizing the Bren gun, he advanced alone, firing the gun from his hip, and mowed down the enemy at point blank range, forcing them to retire in disorder.

"At this point, however, his Company was ordered to withdraw but Corporal Chapman and his section were still left in their advanced position, as the order could not be got forward to them.

"The enemy then began to close up to Corporal Chapman and his isolated section and, under cover of intense machine-gun fire, they made determined charges, with the bayonet. Corporal Chapman again rose with his Bren gun to meet the assaults and on each occasion halted their advance.

"He had now nearly run out of ammunition. Shouting to his section for more bandoliers, he dropped into a fold in the ground and covered those bringing up the ammunition by lying on his back and firing the Bren gun over his shoulder. A party of Germans made every effort to eliminate him with grenades, but with reloaded magazine he closed with them and once again drove the enemy back with considerable casualties.

"During the withdrawal of his Company, the Company Commander had been severely wounded and left lying in the open a short distance from Corporal Chapman. Satisfied that his section was now secure, at any rate for the moment, he went out alone under withering fire and carried his Company Commander for 50 yards to comparative safety. On the way a sniper hit the officer again, wounding Corporal Chapman in the hip and, when he reached our lines, it was discovered that the officer had been killed.

"In spite of his wound, Corporal Chapman refused to be evacuated and went back to his Company until the position was fully restored two hours later.

"Throughout the action Corporal Chapman displayed outstanding gallantry and superb courage. Single-handed he repulsed the attacks of well-led, determined troops and gave his battalion time to reorganise on a vital piece of ground overlooking the only bridge across the canal. His magnificent bravery played a very large part in the capture of this vital ridge and in the successful development of subsequent operations."

He was decorated with the VC by H.M. King George VI at Buckingham Palace, 31st July, 1945.

Citation for the BEM: L.G. 1st June, 1953.

"Sergeant Chapman won the coveted and supreme award for valour for his devotion to duty in the field of battle during the last war. Joining the Territorial Army when it was reformed in 1947, he has taken a full and active part in all the activities of his Company and Battalion. He is the type who is proud to be in the Territorial Army and in addition considers it his duty to serve his country. He was recently taken in for a fourth tour of duty despite the calls of his own business. Unlike many others who sit back and consider they have done their duty, this sergeant is only happy when he is taking part in the activities of the Regiment. I cannot over emphasise what it has meant to his Company and Battalion to have such a man volunteer time and again. His Company has grown in stature by having Sergeant Chapman on its strength."

CAPTAIN IAN LIDDELL
5th Coldstream Guards

Full Name: Ian Oswald Liddell.

Place of Birth: Shanghai, China. The family later resided at Mounton House, Chepstow, Monmouthshire.

Date of Birth: 19th October, 1919.

Father: Percy William Oswald Liddell, J.P.

Mother: Gwendoline Ray Liddell.

Father's Occupation: China Merchant.

Education: St. Andrew's, Eastbourne; Harrow School, April, 1933-July, 1937.

Pre-Service Employment: Trainee Veterinary Surgeon.

Service Record: Enlisted King's Shropshire Light Infantry, 16th May, 1940; RMA Sandhurst; Regular Army Emergency Commission, 2nd Lieutenant, Coldstream Guards, 2nd November, 1940 (Service No. P/156048); member of The Coates Mission at Sandringham House charged with the safety of H.M. King George VI and the Royal Family; Lieutenant, 11th February, 1941; War Substantive Lieutenant, 2nd May, 1942; Temporary Captain, 21st May, 1943; served North West Europe, 1944-45.

Rewards, Decorations and Medals: Victoria Cross (for action near Lingen, Germany, 3rd April, 1945); 1939-45 Star; France and Germany Star; Defence Medal, British War Medal.

Married: Patricia Mary Patton-Bethune, 9th January, 1945, at Kensington, London. She was, at the time, a Section Officer in the W.A.A.F.

Children: None.

Died: K. in A. by a sniper, near Rothenburg, Germany, 21st April, 1945.

Buried: Becklingen War Cemetery, Soltau, Germany, Plot 3, Row D, Grave 13.

Memorials: Becklingen War Cemetery, Soltau, Germany; Mounton Church, Chepstow, Monmouthshire; St. Thomas' Church, Shirenewton, Monmouthshire; Speech Room, Harrow School; Guards Chapel Roll of Honour, Wellington Barracks, London; Liddell Cup presented by his widow to the Coldstreamers' Association (Essex Branch).

Location of VC: Held by the family.

Citation for VC: L.G. 7th June, 1945.

"In Germany on 3rd April, 1945, Captain Liddell was commanding a Company of the Coldstream Guards, which was ordered to capture intact a bridge over the River Ems near Lingen. The bridge was covered on the far bank by an enemy strong point, which was subsequently discovered to consist of 150 entrenched infantry supported by three .88mm and two .20mm guns. The bridge was also prepared for demolition with 500lb bombs which could be plainly seen.

"Having directed his two leading platoons onto the near bank, Captain Liddell ran forward alone to the bridge and scaled the 10 feet high road block guarding it, with the intention of neutralising the charges and taking the bridge intact. In order to achieve this object he had to cross the whole length of the bridge by himself under intense enemy fire, which increased as his object became apparent to the Germans. Having disconnected the charges on the far side, he recrossed the bridge and cut the wires on the near side. It was necessary for him to kneel forming an easy target whilst he successively cut the wires.

"He then discovered that there were also charges underneath the bridge and completely undeterred he also disconnected these. His task completed he then climbed up on to the road block, in full view of the enemy, and signalled his leading platoon to advance.

"Thus alone and unprotected, without cover and under heavy enemy fire, he achieved his object. The bridge was captured intact and the way cleared for the advance across the River Ems. His outstanding gallantry and superb example of courage will never be forgotten by those who saw it.

"This very brave officer has since died of wounds subsequently received in action."

The VC was presented to his widow and mother by H.M. King George VI at Buckingham Palace, 12th February, 1946.

LIEUTENANT COLONEL HERBERT JONES
2nd Parachute Regiment

Full Name: Herbert Jones. He was always known as 'H' Jones.

Place of Birth: Putney, London. The family's address at the time of his birth was 81 Whitehall Court, London, S.W.1. They later resided at Woodbine House, Newry Fawr, Anglesey and The Grange, Kingswear, Devon.

Date of Birth: 14th May, 1940.

Father: Herbert Jones, formerly of Chicago, USA, naturalised British Subject (his father and grandfather had emigrated from Pembrokeshire to the USA in 1851).

Mother: Olwen Jones, daughter of Mr. Pritchard-Jones, J.P., of Holyhead, Anglesey.

Father's Occupation: Gentleman.

Education: St. Peter's School, Seaford, Sussex; Eton College, September, 1953-March, 1958; RMA Sandhurst, September, 1958-April, 1960.

Service Record: Commissioned 2nd Lieutenant, Devonshire and Dorset Regiment, 23rd July, 1960 (Service No. 465788); Lieutenant; transferred to the Parachute Regiment, 10th June, 1965; Captain, 23rd July, 1966; GSO 3 (Operations) January, 1971-March, 1972 at HQ Army Strategic Command; GSO 3 (Operational Planning) April, 1972-August, 1972 at HQ UK Land Forces; Major, 31st December, 1972; transferred to the Devonshire and Dorset Regiment as Company Commander, 1974; transferred to the Parachute Regiment, 1975; served Cyprus, 20th February, 1975-23rd August, 1975; served Belize, 4th November, 1975-16th December, 1975; served Northern Ireland, 30th December, 1975-27th September, 1977 as Brigade Major, 3rd Infantry Brigade; GSO 1 HQ UK Land Forces, August, 1979-April, 1981 (he was intimately involved in the planning and control of UK military participation leading up to the independence of Zimbabwe); Lieutenant Colonel, 1st December, 1979; OC 2nd Battalion The Parachute Regiment, 3rd April, 1981; served Kenya, 5th November, 1981-16th December, 1981; served Belize, 25th January, 1982-12th February, 1982; served Falkland Islands Campaign, 22nd April, 1982-28th May, 1982.

Rewards, Decorations and Medals: Victoria Cross (for action at Darwin and Goose Green, East Falkland Island, 28th May, 1982); OBE (for services with UK Land Forces Staff, L.G. 1st January, 1980); MBE (for services as Brigade Major, 3rd Infantry Brigade, L.G. 1st January, 1977); General Service Medal (clasp for Northern Ireland); South Atlantic Medal (with rosette); Jubilee Medal (1977).

Married: Sara de Uphaugh, 1964. She was a House of Commons Secretary.

Children: Two sons.

Died: K. in A. near Darwin, East Falkland Island, 28th May, 1982.

Buried: Blue Beach War Cemetery, San Carlos Bay, East Falkland Island.

Memorials: Blue Beach War Cemetery, East Falkland Island; Eton College Chapel; Colonel 'H' Jones VC Shell Hole, Sheffield (Memorable Order of Tin Hats).

Location of VC: National Army Museum, Chelsea, London.

Citation for VC: L.G. 8th October, 1982.

"On 28th May, 1982, Lieutenant Colonel Jones was commanding 2nd Battalion The Parachute Regiment on operations on the Falkland Islands.

The Battalion was ordered to attack enemy positions in and around the settlements of Darwin and Goose Green.

"During the attack against an enemy who was well dug in with mutually supporting positions sited in depth, the Battalion was held up just South of Darwin by a particularly well prepared and resilient enemy position of at least eleven trenches on an important ridge. A number of casualties were received. In order to read the battle fully and to ensure that the momentum of his attack was not lost, Colonel Jones took forward his reconnaissance party to the foot of a re-entrant which a section of his Battalion had just secured. Despite persistent, heavy and accurate fire the reconnaissance party gained the top of the re-entrant, at approximately the same height as the enemy positions. From here Colonel Jones encouraged the direction of his Battalion mortar fire, in an effort to neutralise the enemy positions. However these had been well prepared and continued to pour effective fire onto the Battalion advance, which, by now held up for over an hour and under increasingly heavy artillery fire, was in danger of faltering.

"In his effort to gain a good viewpoint, Colonel Jones was now at the very front of his Battalion. It was clear to him that desperate measures were needed in order to overcome the enemy position and rekindle the attack, and that unless these measures were taken promptly the Battalion would sustain increasing casualties and the attack perhaps even fail. It was time for personal leadership and action. Colonel Jones immediately seized a sub-machine gun, and, calling on those around him and with total disregard for his own safety, charged the nearest enemy position. This action exposed him to fire from a number of trenches. As he charged up a short slope at the enemy position he was seen to fall and roll backward downhill. He immediately picked himself up, and again charged the enemy trench, firing his sub-machine gun and seemingly oblivious to the intense fire directed at him. He was hit by fire from another trench which he outflanked, and fell dying only a few feet from the enemy he had assaulted. A short time later a company of the Battalion attacked the enemy, who quickly surrendered. The devastating display of courage by Colonel Jones had completely undermined their will to fight further.

"Thereafter the momentum of the attack was rapidly regained. Darwin and Goose Green were liberated, and the Battalion released the local inhabitants unharmed and forced the surrender of some 1,200 of the enemy.

"The achievements of 2nd Battalion The Parachute Regiment at Darwin and Goose Green set the tone for the subsequent land victory on the Falklands. They achieved such a moral superiority over the enemy in this first battle that, despite the advantages of numbers and selection of battle ground, they never thereafter doubted either the superior fighting qualities of the British troops, or their own inevitable defeat.

"This was an action of the utmost gallantry by a Commanding Officer whose dashing leadership and courage throughout the battle were an inspiration to all about him."

The VC was presented to his widow and sons by H.M. Queen Elizabeth II at Buckingham Palace, 4th November, 1982.

BIBLIOGRAPHY

ABBOTT, P. E. and TAMPLIN, J. M. A., *British Gallantry Awards*, London, Guiness Superlatives Ltd., 1971.

ATKINSON, C. T., *The South Wales Borderers, 24th Foot, 1689-1937*, Cambridge, Regimental History Committee, 1937.

BARCLAY, C. N., *The History of the 53rd (Welsh) Division in the Second World War*, London, William Clowes & Sons, 1956.

BEETON, S. O. (Ed.), *Our Soldiers and the Victoria Cross*, London, Ward, Lock & Tyler, n.d.

BENSON, W. H. D., *Gallant Deeds*, London, Gieves, 1919.

BOWYER, C., *For Valour – The Air VCs*, London, William Kimber, 1978.

BRANCH, N., *Boys' Book of VC Heroes*, London, Publicity Products, 1953.

BULLETIN, THE, Military Historical Society, Various issues.

CAMPBELL, Rear Admiral G., *My Mystery Ships*, London, Hodder & Stoughton, 1928.

CREAGH, General Sir O'Moore, and HUMPHRIS, H. M., *The VC and DSO*, (Vol. 1), London, Standard Art Book Co., 1924.

CROOK, M. J., *The Evolution of the Victoria Cross*, Tunbridge Wells, Midas Books, 1975.

DE COURCY, Captain J., *The History of the Welch Regiment, 1919-1951*, Cardiff, Western Mail & Echo Ltd., 1952.

GORDON, Major L. L., *British Battles and Medals*, (5th Edition), London, Spink & Son, 1979.

GON, P., *The Road to Isandlwana*, Johannesburg, Ad Donker, 1979.

HALL, D., *British Orders, Decorations and Medals*, Huntingdon, Balfour, 1973.

HASTINGS, M., *Men of Glory*, London, Hulton Press, 1958.

ILLUSTRATED LONDON NEWS, Various issues.

JAMESON, Sir W., *Submariner's VC*, London, Peter Davies, 1962.

JOURNAL OF THE ORDERS AND MEDALS RESEARCH SOCIETY, Various issues.

KNOLLYS, W. W., *The Victoria Cross in the Crimea*, London, Dean, 1887.

LEASK, G. A., *VC Heroes of the War*, London, Harrap, 1917.

LUMMIS, Rev. Canon W. M., *Padre George Smith of Rorke's Drift*, Norwich, Lummis, 1978.

LUMMIS FILES, Compiled by the Rev. Canon W. M. Lummis, MC. Held by the Imperial War Museum.

MACINTYRE, D., *Narvik*, London, Evans Brothers, 1959.

MACKINNON, J. P., and SHADBOLT, S., *The South African Campaign, 1879*, London, Hayward, 1973.

MORRIS, D. R., *The Washing of the Spears*, London, Jonathan Cape, 1971.

PARRY, D. H., *Britain's Roll of Glory*, London, Cassell, 1906.

PRATT FILES, Compiled by Mrs. Margaret Pratt. Held by Mr. John Winton.

RANKEN FILES, Held by the Imperial War Museum.

REGISTER OF THE VICTORIA CROSS, Cheltenham, This England Books, 1981.

ROE, F. G., *The Bronze Cross,* London, Gawthorn, 1945.

SMYTH, Brigadier The Hon. Sir J., *The Story of the Victoria Cross, 1856-1963,* London, Muller, 1963.

SOLDIERS OF THE QUEEN, journal of the Victorian Military Society, Various issues.

STEWART, R., *The Victoria Cross: The Empire's Roll of Valour,* London, Hutchinson, 1928.

SWETTENHAM, J., *Valiant Men: Canada's VC and GC Winners,* London, Seeley Service & Cooper, 1975.

TOOMEY, T. E., *The Victoria Cross and How Won,* London, Boot, 1890.

UYS, I. S., *For Valour – The History of Southern Africa's Victoria Cross Heroes,* Johannesburg, Uys, 1973.

WAR ILLUSTRATED, Various issues.

WARD, Major C. H. D., *Regimental Records of the Royal Welch Fusiliers (23rd Foot),* London, Forster Groom & Co., various dates during the 1920s.

WHITEHORN, Major A. C. and MARDEN, Major General Sir T. O., *The History of the Welch Regiment,* Cardiff, Western Mail & Echo Ltd., 1932.

WHITTON, F. E., *Rorke's Drift,* booklet reprinted from Blackwood's Magazine, January, 1979.

WIGMORE, L., and HARDING, B., *They Dared Mightily,* Canberra, Australian War Memorial, 1963.

WILKINS, P. A., *The History of the Victoria Cross,* London, Constable, 1904.

WINTON, J., *The Victoria Cross at Sea,* London, Michael Joseph, 1979.

1. Major Luke O'Connor, VC., c.1874.
2. Major General Luke O'Connor, VC., c.1906.
3. Major General Sir Luke O'Connor, VC., with the Royal Welch Fusiliers regimental mascot, c.1913.
4. Artist's impression of Captain Edward Bell's VC action.

5. Colonel Edward Bell, VC., c.1865.
6. Colour Sergeant Ambrose Madden, VC., taken in the camp at Sebastopol, 1856. This is believed to be a photograph of this man but no officially identified picture of him exists.
7. Brevet Major Hugh Rowlands, VC., (standing, leaning on his sword), taken in the camp at Sebastopol, 1856.
8. Major Hugh Rowlands, VC., c.1860.

9. Major General Hugh Rowlands, VC., c.1882.
10. General Sir Hugh Rowlands, VC., in retirement, outside the lodge to his home at Plastirion, c.1905.
11. Plastirion, Llanrug, the home of General Sir Hugh Rowlands, VC., c.1907.

12

13

14

15

12. Rear Admiral Henry Raby, VC., c.1900.
13. Lieutenant Charles Lumley, c.1850.
14. Surgeon William Sylvester, VC., c.1871.
15. Dr. William Sylvester, VC., c.1900.

16. Artist's impression of Corporal Robert Shields' VC action.
17. Lt. General Sir James Hills-Johnes, VC., c.1900.
18. Captain, Hon. Augustus Anson, VC., c.1860.
19. Lt. Colonel, Hon. Augustus Anson, VC., c.1870.

20. Lt. Colonel Thomas Hackett, VC., c.1874.
21. Private George Monger, VC., c.1861.
22. Thomas Monaghan, VC., c.1875.
23. Charles Anderson. VC., c.1870.

24. Campbell Douglas (standing) with his brother Archibald, c.1850.
25. Assistant Surgeon Campbell Douglas, c.1862.
26. Assistant Surgeon Campbell Douglas, c.1864.
27. Surgeon Major Campbell Douglas, VC., c.1876.

28. Surgeon Lt. Colonel Campbell Douglas, VC., on the beach at Dover, June, 1895, after having crossed the English Channel in a 12-foot Canadian canoe.
29. Surgeon Lt. Colonel Campbell Douglas, VC., in his patented collapsible canoe, c.1899.

30. Surgeon Lt. Colonel Campbell Douglas, VC., (seated left) with his
brother, Admiral Archibald Douglas, at Portsmouth, c.1905.
31. David Bell, VC., c.1900 (see also picture 53).
32. Thomas Murphy, VC., c.1880.

33. Lieutenant Lord Gifford, VC., c.1874.
34. Lieutenant Teignmouth Melvill, c.1879.
35. Artist's impression of Lieutenant Teignmouth Melvill's escape from
    Isandlwana, 1879.
36. Lieutenant Nevill Coghill, c.1876.

37. Lieutenant Nevill Coghill, c.1878.
38. Lieutenant Gonville Bromhead, c.1872.
39. Sergeant William Allan, VC., c.1880.
40. Sergeant Instructor William Allan, VC., c.1885.

41. Private Frederick Hitch, VC., 1879. His arm is in a sling recovering from the wound which he received during the defence of Rorke's Drift.
42. Frederick Hitch, VC., in the uniform of the Corps of Commissionaires, c.1880.
43. Frederick Hitch VC., c.1900.
44. Private William Jones, VC., 1879.

45. William Jones, VC., c.1905 (see also picture 53).
46. Private Robert Jones, VC., 1879 (see also picture 53).
47. Private Henry Hook, VC., 1879 (see also picture 53).
48. Sergeant Henry Hook, VC., c.1890.

49. The grave of Sergeant Henry Hook, VC.
50. Private John Williams, VC., 1879.
51. Sergeant John Williams, VC., c.1900 (see also picture 53).
52. Major Edward Browne, VC., c.1885 (see also picture 53).

53. A rare photograph of the VCs of the 24th Regiment of Foot, c.1895. Standing (L-R) Robert Jones, VC., Sergeant Henry Hook, VC., William Jones VC., Sitting (L-R) David Bell, VC., Colonel Edward Browne, VC., Frederick Hitch, VC., Corporal John Williams, VC.
54. John Doogan, VC., c.1893.
55. Lance Corporal Samuel Vickery, VC., c.1901.

56

57

58

59

56. Captain Nevill Smyth, VC., c.1897.
57. Private Charles Ward, VC., recovering from the wound he received in his VC action.
58. Private Charles Ward, VC., c.1900.
59. Lieutenant Llewelyn Price-Davies, c.1899.

60

61

62

60. Major General and Mrs Price-Davies at the Odney Club, Cookham, c.1939.
61. Major General Llewelyn Price-Davies, VC., c.1959.
62. Marrington Hall, Chirbury, Shropshire, the birthplace of Major General Llewelyn Price-Davies, VC.

63. Artist's impression of Lance Corporal William Fuller's VC action.
64. Lance Corporal William Fuller, VC., 1915. (see also picture 99).
65. Able Seaman William C. Williams, c.1915.

66. Artist's impression of Able Seaman William C. Williams, VC action. The
figure on the left of the picture is Commander Unwin VC.
67. The parents of Able Seaman William C. Williams, VC. His Father is
wearing the VC which he had just received from HM King George V.
68. Lieutenant Colonel Charles Doughty Wylie, c.1915.

69. Company Sergeant Major Frederick Barter, VC., 1915.
70. Lieutenant Frederick Barter, VC., c.1918
71. Rupert Hallowes, c.1890.
72. Rupert Hallowes, c.1895.

73. Private Rupert Hallowes, c.1914.
74. Sergeant Samuel Meekosha, VC., c.1916.
75. Officer Cadet Samuel Meekosha, VC., with members of his family and friends, 1917.
76. Major Samuel Ingham, VC. (formerly Meekosha), 1944.

77. Lieutenant Edgar Myles, VC., 1917.
78. Lieutenant Angus Buchanan, c.1916.
79. Captain Angus Buchanan, VC., c.1930. The severe head wounds which blinded him are clearly visible in this picture.
80. Private James Finn, 1916.

81. Lieutenant Lionel Rees, c.1914.
82. Wing Commander Lionel Rees, VC., holding the Sword of Honour
    presented to him by the town and people of Caernarfon in January, 1920.
83. Wing Commander Lionel Rees, VC., RAF Fencing Champion, 1923.
84. Group Captain Lionel Rees, VC., aboard his ketch *May* in the Bahamas
    after his single-handed crossing of the Atlantic Ocean in 1933.

85. Captain Lionel Rees' DH2 after a crash landing in 1916. This was the aircraft in which he won the Military Cross.
86. Members of 32 Squadron, RFC, 26 May, 1916. Lionel Rees is seated in the middle row, second from the right.

87

88

87. Members of the Balfour Mission with their hosts at the Detroit Athletic Club, July, 1917. Lionel Rees is the centre figure.
88. Sergeant Joseph Davies, VC., (centre) with two Military Medal winners of the Royal Welch Fusiliers, c.1916.

89. Private Joseph Davies, whilst serving with the Welch Regiment in Egypt, c.1913.
90. Sergeant Joseph Davies, VC., recovering from the wounds which he received during the 2nd Battle of Ypres. This picture was taken on the day that he was invested with the VC at Buckingham Palace.
91. Regimental Sergeant Major Joseph Davies, VC., with his daughter Victoria, during the Second World War.
92. Joseph Davies, VC., (centre) shortly before his death.

93. Private Albert Hill, VC., c.1916
94. Albert Hill, VC., with his wife aboard the *Queen Elizabeth* en route for the 1956 VC Reunion.
95. Albert Hill, VC., c.1956.
96. Private Hubert Lewis, c.1915.

97. Hubert Lewis, VC., c.1939 (see also pictures 99 and 158).
98. Sergeant Albert White, c.1916. This very poor newspaper print is the only known picture of this man.
99. (L-R), Ivor Rees, VC., William Fuller, VC., Hubert Lewis, VC., c.1965.

100

101

102

103

100. Leading Seaman William Williams, VC., c.1917.
101. Leading Seaman William Williams, VC., arriving at Llangefni, Anglesey, 31st October, 1918, where he was honoured as the county's most decorated serviceman of the Great War.
102. William Williams, VC., c.1938 as Standard Bearer of the Holyhead British Legion. .
103. Private James Davies, c.1914, in the uniform of the Royal Garrison Artillery.

104. Private Robert Bye, c.1915 (the rank of Guardsman was not introduced
  until after the Great War).
105. Sergeant Ivor Rees, VC., September, 1918.
106. Ivor Rees, VC., with his wife and children, 1925.

107

108

109

110

107. Ivor Rees, VC., with his wife at the VC Centenary Exhibition,
Marlborough House, 1956 (see also picture 158).
108. Frederick Birks (the small boy standing behind the vicar) as a member of
the Buckley Boys Brigade, c.1908.
109. Private Frederick Birks, c.1915.
110. 2nd Lieutenant Frederick Birks, 1917. This is a retouched photograph to
which the VC has been added at a later date.

111. Private John Collins, c.1915.
112. Officer Cadet Lewis Evans, 1899.
113. Temporary Brigadier General Lewis Evans,VC., c.1918.
114. Colonel Lewis Evans, VC., c.1932.

115

116

117

118

115. Brigadier Lewis Evans, VC., c.1960.
116. Captain John Fox Russell, c.1916.
117. Captain Richard Wain, c.1916.
118. Arthur Lascelles, c.1914.

119

120

121

122

119. Captain Arthur Lascelles, VC., 1918.
120. 2nd Lieutenant Thomas Pryce, 1917.
121. Lance Corporal Henry Weale, VC., (front left) in Scotland recovering
     from his wounds, 1918.
122. Sergeant Henry Weale, VC., c.1921.

123. Henry Weale, VC., leaving Rhyl Station en route for the VC Centenary Reunion, 1956.

124. Chief Petty Officer George Prowse, c.1918.

125. William Waring (front centre) with his workmates at Mr Bushell's Poultry Works, Welshpool, c.1913.

126. Sergeant William Waring (left) Montgomeryshire Yeomanry, c.1913.

127. The parents, brothers and sisters of Lance Sergeant William Waring, VC., leaving Buckingham Palace after receiving his VC, 8th March, 1919.

128. Sergeant William Waring whilst training at Cromer, 1916.

129. Private Allan Lewis, c.1915.

130. Company Sergeant Major John H. Williams, VC., c.1919, still recovering from the severe wounds which he received in 1918.
131. Company Sergeant Major John H. Williams, VC., c.1919.
132. John H. Williams, VC., in the uniform of a commissionaire at the Steel, Iron and Coal Company, Ebbw Vale, c.1925 (see also picture 157).
133. William Bissett (kneeling) as a member of Crief Town Band, c.1908.

134. Lieutenant William Bissett, VC., c.1919.
135. Major Dudley Johnson, c.1918.
136. Captain Dudley Johnson with his wife and son c.1915.
137. Temporary Lieutenant Colonel Dudley Johnson, VC., leaving
Buckingham Palace with his son after receiving the VC, Bar to the DSO
and the MC, 14th June, 1919.

138. Major General Dudley Johnson, VC., conducting HM King George VI at an inspection at Aldershot, c.1940.

139. Major General Dudley Johnson, VC., c. 1973 (see also picture 157).

140. Private Samuel Pearse, c.1915.

141. Bernard Warburton-Lee (back row, second from the left), in the Malvern Link Prep School Cricket Team, c.1908.

142. Lieutenant Bernard Warburton-Lee, c.1918.
143. Lieutenant Commander Bernard Warburton-Lee with his wife and son, 1927.
144. Captain Bernard Warburton-Lee, c.1939.
145. 2nd Lieutenant the Hon. Christopher Furness, c.1938.

146. Flight Lieutenant Hughie Edwards, c.1941.
147. Air Commodore Sir Hughie Edwards, VC., c.1980.
148. Squadron Leader Hughie Edwards, VC., with the Australian Prime
     Minister, c.1943.

149

150

151

152

149. Lieutenant Commander Stephen Beattie, c.1942.
150. Commander John Linton, c.1942.
151. Major Tasker Watkins, VC., 1944.
152. The Hon. Lord Justice Watkins, VC., 1983.

153. Flight Lieutenant David Lord (right), 1943.
154. Flight Lieutenant David Lord, 1944.
155. Corporal Edward Chapman, VC., 1945.
156. Corporal Edward Chapman, VC., and his father visiting Ogilvy Colliery, 1945.

157

158

157. (L-R) Company Sergeant Major John H. Williams, VC., Corporal Edward Chapman, VC., Major General Dudley Johnson, VC., 1945.
158. (L-R) Edward Chapman, VC., Mrs Chapman, Ivor Rees, VC., Hubert Lewis, VC., at the showing of the feature film *Zulu* to the South Wales Borderers in the early 1960s.

159. Company Sergeant Major Edward Chapman, VC., c.1956.
160. Captain Ian Liddell (left) talking with the first men across the Ems River
     after his VC action, 3 April, 1945.
161. 'H' Jones with his father c.1946.
162. 2nd Lieutenant 'H' Jones, 1960.

163   164

165

163. Major 'H' Jones with his wife and sons at Buckingham Palace after
     receiving the MBE in 1977.
164. Lieutenant Colonel 'H' Jones at the helm of his yacht, c.1981.
165. Lieutenant Colonel 'H' Jones on exercise with the Parachute Regiment,
     c.1981.

166

167

166. Lieutenant Colonel 'H' Jones at the wheel of his racing Bentley.
167. Lieutenant Colonel 'H' Jones (centre) aboard a landing craft at Ascension Island, en route for the Falkland Islands, 1982.

Unless otherwise indicated below, the pictures contained in this book are from the author's own collection.